John Brown

A Cry for Freedom

John Brown

A Cry for Freedom

by Lorenz Graham

ILLUSTRATED WITH PHOTOGRAPHS

THOMAS Y. CROWELL | NEW YORK

Photo Acknowledgments

Courtesy of Library of Congress: photo on front cover, pp. 111, 113, 117, 129, 134, 158, 162.

Courtesy of Milton Meltzer: photo on back cover, pp. 5, 17, 21, 22, 32, 38, 40, 56, 63, 78, 81, 87, 93, 132, 138, 142, 151, 155, 159.

Maps prepared by Frank Aloise.

BT 9.95 / 6 14 -1/81

Library of Congress Cataloging in Publication Data

Graham, Lorenz B
  John Brown, a cry for freedom.

  Includes index.
  SUMMARY: A biography of the controversial abolitionist who played a role in the northward movement of runaway slaves and led the raid on Harpers Ferry.
    1. Brown, John, 1800–1859—Juvenile literature.
  2. Abolitionists—United States—Biography—Juvenile literature. [1. Brown, John, 1800–1859. 2. Abolitionists] I. Title.
E451.G74   1980   973.6′8′0924 [B] [92] 79–7903
ISBN 0-690-04023-7
ISBN 0-690-04024-5 (lib. bdg.)

Y A B
Brown
Gr

1 2 3 4 5 6 7 8 9 10
First Edition

I humbly trust that my death will not be in vain.
God can make it to be a thousand times more valuable
in His cause than all the miserable service, at best,
that I have rendered.

From John Brown's
letter to his children,
November 22, 1859

Contents

[vii]

Introduction

Many stories have been written about John Brown.
He has been praised as a defender of the rights of
man. He has been denounced as a butcher of men. He
has been scorned as a fanatic, a foolish white man who
was willing to die in fighting to make black people free.

At Harpers Ferry in 1859 John Brown and his men
took direct action to end slavery. In the fighting some
of his men were killed. Others were captured with
Brown. Those who were taken alive were tried and condemned in a court of law, and they were all hanged.

Some say the action at Harpers Ferry was really the
beginning of the Civil War, which tore the country apart
from 1861 to 1865. The story of John Brown became
a legend. For years after his death men went into battle
singing

John Brown's body lies a mouldering in the grave
But his soul goes marching on!

[ix]

The story of John Brown and his cry for freedom is now given again because his life did indeed help to make this country what it is today, and his beliefs, his words, and his prophecies apply to present conditions.

We need to share Brown's view of the destructive aspects of slavery. Then we will recognize the self-poisoning effects of race hatred. We need to know why he so willingly died. Then we will understand why today some men and women are willing to give their lives in the struggle for social justice.

When John Brown was born in 1800, the United States of America was a new country. It was growing up, and John Brown grew up with it.

He saw that the development of wealth in his country depended on the labor of slaves. Africans had been imported and forced to work without pay. Laws identified these people and their descendants as slaves, property to be bought and sold and to be bred for profit like animals.

Many people believed that it was not right to hold human beings as property; still they recognized that slavery was very profitable. Everyone knew that the nation at its beginning was dedicated to the proposition that all men are created equal and that they are endowed by their creator with the right to life, liberty, and the pursuit of happiness. Very few people believed that these fine words should apply to the slaves.

John Brown was one who did believe that the proposition set forth in the Declaration of Independence applied to all men, black as well as white. He believed that slavery was an evil which would, like cancer, destroy the nation. He and some others believed that the unpaid labor of slaves was a threat to the wage-earning labor of free men. He looked ahead, and he saw with the eyes of a prophet that sooner or later slavery would have to be given up.

The Emancipation Proclamation resolved the issue of slavery in America three years after the death of John Brown, but the proposition that all men are created equal is not yet fully accepted.

Some people still believe that members of their own race are inherently superior to members of other races. In America some white people want to keep black people in a separate and unequal status. Those who struggle for full equality in education and employment meet resistance not only in words but also in the form of violence.

After reading about John Brown and the conditions in his day, we will better understand some of the problems with which we still have to deal.

John Brown

A Cry for Freedom

1

John Brown Grows Strong and Hardy

John Brown was born into a family of strong early Americans. Their strength of character shaped the life of young John. He was a direct descendant of one of the company who came from England on the Mayflower in 1620.

His grandfather, also named John Brown, fought against the British in the Continental Army. In the winter of 1776 he died while in that service. His family was destitute. There was no pension. One of his eleven children was five-year-old Owen, who grew up to become the father of our John Brown.

At the age of twelve Owen worked with a shoemaker to learn the trade. He received little more than his food and a place to sleep. At sixteen he set out on his own, moving frequently from place to place making and mending shoes and harnesses. At the age of twenty-two Owen married Ruth Mills, daughter of a minister. For a while he was quite successful in his work. He was able to buy a place of his own in Norfolk, Connecticut.

Owen was outspoken in his opposition to slavery. He remembered that after his father died, some kind friends sent their slave to the Brown home to help with the plowing. After work the slave carried Owen on his back. The boy loved the slave, and he was saddened when the slave sickened and died. Later he heard sermons preached against the practice of slavery. He believed slavery was a great sin, and he was glad when Connecticut abolished slavery by law in 1784.

Both Owen and Ruth were sober, hardworking, and pious. Their first two children died while they were very young, and the parents believed they were being punished for something. Indeed, Owen thought he had been too proud of his success as a tanner and cobbler.

After another child was born, a girl named Anna, Owen sold his house and bought a small farm near West Torrington, Connecticut, where John Brown was born on May 9, 1800.

Life on the rocky piece of land was hard for the Brown family. Owen Brown earned practically nothing at his trade of tanning and cobbling. Those around him had little if any money to pay him. Some of his neighbors were moving to the Western Reserve lands beyond the Allegheny Mountains. It was spoken of as "way out west." Wild game roamed the prairies. Indians, some of whom were hostile, outnumbered the white settlers.

In 1804 Owen Brown journeyed out into Ohio, which had been admitted to the Union the previous year. He selected a piece of land in the settlement of Hudson, some twenty-five miles south of Cleveland, and returned to his family.

The next summer the Browns sold the property in

**The house in Torrington, Connecticut, where John Brown
was born on May 9, 1800.**

Connecticut. With a neighbor family they loaded their furniture and equipment in wagons drawn by teams of oxen and set out for Ohio. They took with them their livestock, horses, and cows. It proved to be a great and happy experience for five-year-old John.

In later years John wrote about that trip. He said it was rich in learning experiences. His father let him help, and he "learned to think he could accomplish smart things in driving the cows and riding the horses."

The trail led the small wagon train from Connecticut across New York state with a ferry crossing of the Hudson River. John saw something of the Catskill Mountains. Later, as they moved through wide Pennsylvania, the trail followed swift-flowing streams at times, and it led up and over the mountain ridges of the Appalachians and the Alleghenies.

John was excited at the sight of wild animals. Some of them were shot for food. He was told to be wary of bears, but they did not come near the wagon train. There were many snakes—rattlers and copperheads. He killed them when he could, and he was always on guard.

The sight of Indians terrified him. He had heard about attacks and massacres. Men described the native Americans as savages and often boasted about having killed redskins.

John heard one of the experienced men talking to Owen Brown.

"You'll only see one at a time," he said, "but you always know there be more out there. The ones you see are the look-outs, spies for the others, trying to figure what we're going to do, and how strong we are and like that."

John's father replied, "But they tell me the Indians only attack when they believe we're trying to take from them. Like it's been in the East. Our people have come in and taken over the land, to farm it and to settle it with our towns and cities."

"Well I guess we got the right to take over. They don't own the land. They got no title. They don't farm it. They don't build cities."

"I perceive," said Owen Brown, "that God is no respecter of persons. Be they white or red, or even black, they're all God's creatures, and the white man's got no right to rob them or to make slaves of them. And if we do, then they got every right to fight back at us."

The trip was a great adventure for John, but after they reached Hudson, the family faced a difficult year. It was too late in the season to make a crop. Their house was a drafty log cabin. Through fall and winter John shivered with the sharp winds, the driving rains, and the heavy snows. The family subsisted on some wild game and on food "borrowed" from neighbors who had scarcely enough for themselves. In the spring they cleared and planted. Birds and squirrels ravaged their crop, then a late freeze destroyed what little the creatures had left.

After the first hard year their circumstances improved. John's father earned some money at tanning leather and making shoes and harnesses. Young John learned to cure the skins of deer, rabbits, and squirrels, as well as the hides of sheep and cattle. He followed his father at the tasks, and he helped whenever he could. His clothes were made of buckskin.

When he first arrived in Ohio, John was afraid of Indians, but after a few contacts with them, he lost his fears. One of the boys became his friend. He was taller than John and perhaps older. Neither of them knew the language of the other, but they liked to be together. John learned that his new friend's name was Leesolu and that his people were of the Seneca tribe or nation. John liked to spend time in the woods and on the grassy hills and in the valleys around Hudson. Leesolu would go with him.

The first time they stopped to drink at a bubbling, clear stream John made his friend know the word "water," and John learned what Leesolu said for water. So they learned other words, as "man" and "horse," and useful verbs such as "go," "come," and "eat." With a few words and many signs and gestures they could understand each other.

For several days John missed seeing his friend. Then one morning, while he ran alone across the prairie, Leesolu came up silently and ran beside him. Neither spoke, but John felt it was good to have his friend with him again. Leesolu sprinted ahead. He took the lead, and when he turned toward the right, John followed. Their way led up a gentle slope that became a hill. At the top of the incline Leesolu stopped with John beside him. They looked across a wide valley where a party of Indians was moving. Their few horses were heavily loaded, and most of the people walked bent beneath heavy packs.

Without uttering words, but using signs and gestures, Leesolu made John know that those were his people and that they were leaving for some distant place. Leesolu put his hand into a leather pouch, which he wore on a thong at his waist, and took from it a small, shining yellow ball.

For the first time he spoke.

"John," he said as he put the ball in John's hand.

He turned and ran swiftly toward the moving figures.

The shining ball was a thing of beauty. It was like a large marble of highly polished stone. John recognized it as a gift of friendship. He stayed on the hill until he saw Leesolu merge into the group with his people and they, with him, were lost to sight as they moved across another ridge.

John made for himself a leather pouch like the one Leesolu had worn, and in this he carried his treasure. Those who saw it admired it.

"I have never seen anything like it," his mother said. "It is like a jewel."

Older boys and men who saw it wanted to buy it or

to trade for it. John could not think of giving it up; he was proud of this unusual possession. He often carried it in his hand. When he ran with it across the prairie, it was almost as though Leesolu were running with him. While he was working, he sometimes placed it where he could see it.

His father spoke harshly about the ball and John's admiration of it.

"It is only a thing," Owen Brown told his son. "Be careful. You should not love it. I see you looking at it with worship in your eyes. None but God Himself is worthy of such adoration, and the Lord thy God is a jealous god . . . thou shalt have no other before Him."

Perhaps John had some feelings of guilt. He tried to keep his father from knowing how deeply he felt about this symbol of his friend.

Then one day the yellow ball was lost.

John searched in all the places he thought it might be. The leather pouch was empty. The ball was not in any other pocket. He shook his bedclothes, and it did not fall out. John went about the places where he had been working, and he looked under and behind the scant furnishings in the house.

He later wrote that the loss was a great sorrow for him and that when he was alone he cried.

Shortly after losing the yellow stone John caught a young squirrel. He was severely bitten by the frantic animal, and the squirrel lost his tail in his unsuccessful attempt to get away. However, the squirrel was tamed, and he became an ever-present pet. John called him Bob Tail. He fed him and protected him from dogs and from people who might have hurt him. Bob Tail did not learn to do any tricks, but he liked to stay close to John. When John went away from home or away from his father's place, Bob Tail would ride in John's pocket.

This treasure John also lost. The little animal could have been killed, or it may simply have run away to be with its kind in the woods. Young John mourned his loss, and for years after, each time he saw a squirrel he looked to see if it had a stubby tail.

The separation from his Indian friend, the loss of the yellow marblelike ball, and the loss of his pet all combined to reinforce the teaching of John's pious father. He did not try to get another pet. He felt that anything that he really liked very much would be taken away from him by a jealous god. He was yet to suffer the greatest loss of his young life.

His mother, as well as his father, was a stern and deeply religious person whose love exhibited itself in bringing up her children "in the fear and admonition of the Lord." She believed that punishment was of God and that liars stood in danger of hellfire. John was her liveliest and most promising child. She loved him and wanted to correct his faults. She frequently punished him with lashes of switches and leather straps. John took the lashings without resentment. He loved his mother, and he was sure that she really cared for him.

John was eight years old when his mother and her newborn baby died. The whole family was grief-stricken. John believed he would never recover from a loss so complete and permanent. Owen Brown, unable to cope with the task of raising six young children, sought and found a young woman willing to marry him and carry on the family responsibilities. She was only twenty years old, and although she proved to be a good wife and mother, John refused to accept her emotionally. He mourned and pined for his own mother for several years. His three early sorrows and his growing up without a good mother relationship must have affected his character as an adult.

Not all of John's childhood was sad. His father sent him to the local school, but John was not studious. He did not like school. He preferred to be at work with his father. However, he was smart, and at home and in school he learned rapidly and well. By the time he was ten years old he was reading well. A friend of his father recognized his ability and persuaded him to read history. He offered the use of his library. From that time on, reading formed the base of his education, and books of history were his favorites.

John liked to work with his father, and he learned the skills of tanning. But even more than being with his father, John loved to spend time in the woods and on the grassy hills and in the wide valleys around Hudson. In warm weather he would be seen walking or sometimes running through the country in buckskin shirt and pants, barefooted and bareheaded. In colder weather he hunted and trapped. He knew the country, and he knew the ways of animals.

He grew strong and sturdy, thin but tall for his age. With other boys he enjoyed only the roughest of play, especially wrestling. He developed early his ability to get out of trouble, to explain away his mistakes, and what later he described as a mean habit of telling lies to screen himself from blame. He seemed to be afraid of nothing.

2

Brown Forms His Own Opinions

In addition to his work as a tanner, John's father developed business as a dealer in cattle. During the War of 1812 he supplied beef to the federal troops. Herds of cattle had to be driven through the country. At the age of 12 John was large and he was a good worker. He accompanied his father on cattle drives, and he soon learned to do the whole job by himself. Alone, he could take a herd a hundred miles and more. His father trusted him. Businessmen and army officers commended him.

John was still young when he decided that he would excel in whatever he did. He was always alert, observing everything and forming his own opinions. From what he saw of the officers and men of the army he developed a strong dislike for military affairs.

At that time Ohio was a "free" state. Buying and selling of human beings was not permitted there. Some free blacks lived in Ohio, and some white people continued to use blacks as slaves. John's travels with cattle took him across the Ohio River into Kentucky, where slavery was legal. On one of these trips he was in the home of a United States marshall who owned a black boy. This slave was about the same age as John. John saw that the boy worked hard and that he was smart. The two boys talked together. John believed they could have become friends, but he realized that their lives were very different.

The slave owner praised John and showed him every kindness. But he abused the slave, cursing him and striking him for any slight mistake. The boy was fed only scraps of food and very little of it. He was scarcely clothed at all. At one time John watched in silent horror as the master beat the boy with an iron shovel.

Later in the day the marshall talked to John about the incident.

"Guess you were surprised at what you saw this morning," he said. "But you're not used to dealing with slaves and training them."

"Yes, sir. You're right," John answered. "I was brought up to think the Africans are people same as we are, and that it's a sin to use them as slaves."

The marshall laughed. Then he became serious.

"That's where you're wrong, boy," he said. "Firstly, these blacks are not people, and next, it's God's law they be slaves for us. Why, that's in the Bible. And to train a slave you got to beat him. That lazy boy has it easy around here. He don't have much to do. If you didn't beat the niggers they wouldn't work, and pretty soon they wouldn't want to be slaves. Pretty soon they'd be fighting back or running off."

"But, sir," John said when he had the chance, "it looked like you were trying to kill him."

"Oh, no," the marshall said. "You don't kill a slave. Might be he thought he was getting killed. That's alright. And he knows he could be killed. He's my property and I got the right, but yet and still he is property and he's worth money. I wasn't about to kill him. You saw him walking around when I got through with him. I never broke a bone in his body. I was right careful about that. But I have to beat him. I beat him regular. He's got to be kept scared. You'll see how it is. And the more you beat the niggers while they're young the less you have to beat them when they grow up."

John never forgot that slave boy, and he never forgot that slave owner.

When the war was over and John's father turned his attention again to the tanning of leather, John worked full time in the tannery. He developed not only skills needed in the work but also the ability to supervise others, all of whom were older than he was.

From all that he saw and all that he read, John grew to admire strength and courage and to dislike weakness and cowardice. He enjoyed books of history and books about the lives of great and wise and good men. He read the Bible and became familiar with it. He could quote long passages, whole chapters, and sometimes whole books of the Bible. Like most of the people around him, he believed that the Bible was the holy word of a very personal God. He believed that everything in the Bible was literally true. He believed that God was able to talk directly to men, and he hoped that some day God would speak to him.

He had his share of problems. He realized that he

was lacking in some elements of education. Although he had read widely in history and in the Bible, he had neglected the study of arithmetic, so he set about to learn mathematics, and he studied surveying. Mastering this work further increased his confidence.

Those who worked with him considered him arrogant. He gave his instructions as though they were military commands. He demanded excellence, and he would not allow a job to be poorly done. He also developed a habit of lying, and he shouted down and threatened any who challenged him. With men and boys he was bold and self-confident, but with girls he was painfully shy and uncomfortable.

At one time he began to question religious beliefs such as his father held, but his doubts did not last. At the age of sixteen he was admitted to membership in the Congregational Church of Hudson, and soon after that he decided God wanted him to be a preacher. Preparing for such a career would take time and serious study. John was willing to pay that price, but to prepare for college he had to study at night. His eyes were not good. Reading by the light of candles was a great strain, and there were no good eyeglasses at that time. He had to give up the idea of college and of the ministry as a career.

For the next several years he continued to work in the business of tanning for his father, and later in a tannery which he and a partner set up outside the village. The business did well. On his own account he bought and sold cattle. Then he developed an interest in sheep, and added to his profits with the wool they produced. Later he became an expert in wool production and a leader among farmers of the area.

At the age of twenty John Brown married Dianthe Lusk, whom he described as "a remarkably plain but neat and industrious and economical girl of excellent character, earnest piety and good practical common sense." They started a family and soon had several children.

For a short while the business of tanning and the dealing in cattle and sheep provided a comfortable living for Brown's young family. His success in business gave him great satisfaction. Perhaps it also intensified his religious feelings. He lived by strict rules, and he held his employees and members of his family in the bonds of strict discipline. Church attendance was compulsory for all who worked for him. In addition, he required all of them to join him every morning in prayer at his house.

His wife, Dianthe, sickened. He believed a change would be good for her, so he sold his home and his business in Hudson, Ohio. He moved eastward, buying a two-hundred-acre tract in the wilderness of northwest Pennsylvania. The family settled there in 1826.

It looked like a good move. Brown was welcomed in the new community, and he became a leader. He built a large house and a barn with a secret room for hiding runaway slaves. He set up a tannery, the first industry in that area. He started a school in which he took his turn as teacher, and he helped to get a post office for what was called Richmond Township. He was the postmaster from 1828 to 1835.

In the year 1831 the family ran into a series of reverses. John himself was sick with a fever that sapped his strength and made it impossible for him to work. One of his sons died. Then his wife, Dianthe, became sick with fever. Some say she lost her mind. She bore her seventh child, which did not live, and she died on August 10, 1832.

For a long time John Brown's health did not return. He lost his tanning business. Nothing seemed to turn out as he planned it.

A year after Dianthe died, John married again. His new wife, Mary Day, was only seventeen years old at the time, but she cheerfully took on the task of mothering the five Brown children. In the years that followed, Mary Day Brown added seven sons and six daughters to the family.

In 1835, with his financial condition no better, Brown borrowed money and moved back to Ohio, establishing a home at Franklin Mills, a village near Hudson.

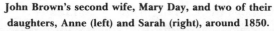

John Brown's second wife, Mary Day, and two of their daughters, Anne (left) and Sarah (right), around 1850.

3

"I Consecrate My Life"

Although Brown had business and family troubles, he was always involved in the antislavery movement. He was an alert observer, and he read the words of leaders in the nation. His own father had talked about slavery as a great sin. Brown taught that a righteous God would punish sinners. Also, he saw the institution of slavery as a threat to the ideals of America.

William Lloyd Garrison said in his paper *The Liberator*, an antislavery journal, that the statement "all men are created equal" included black as well as white men and that black as well as white were endowed with the right to "life, liberty, and the pursuit of happiness." To this John Brown heartily agreed. He had seen some of the evils of slavery on his visits southward out of Ohio. He had seen runaway slaves moving northward trying to reach the safety of Canada.

From his reading he knew that the first Africans were imported in 1619 at Jamestown, Virginia. They were indentured servants. That is, after working for seven years, they were free to leave the person for whom they had worked. In this way many white people came to the colonies from Europe. Indentured servants who were white left their masters after seven years and merged with other Europeans. Soon they would be living like other free citizens. They would be lost in the general population. Because they were black, Africans were readily identifiable. Their masters found ways of keeping the Africans in service. One way was to claim the servant owed money. Another was to say the servant had misbehaved and therefore owed more time. Masters used many ways of keeping control of their free labor.

Then the laws were changed. In 1662 the colony of Virginia declared that black Africans in service were slaves. They were to be treated as property, to be bought and sold. All new babies would be the property of the master of the mother. Other colonies made similar slave laws.

In the Revolutionary War thousands of black men, in the South as well as in the North, gained their freedom by military or naval service, fighting for the freedom and liberty of the colonists.

After the United States was formed, the beautiful words of the Declaration of Independence and of the Constitution made some people see the injustice of slavery. In 1787 the Congress passed laws prohibiting slavery in the Western Reserve lands north of the Ohio River. At about this time the northern states were adopting similar laws for their areas. The population of free blacks increased rapidly.

The labor of slaves was very important to the large plantations of the South. More hands were needed all the time. The more slaves a planter had, the more land he could buy. The more land he bought, the more slaves he needed. Wealth was built on the ownership of slaves, who worked at very little cost to the owner.

Thousands more Africans were imported. Slave trade added to the wealth of northern shipbuilders and ship-owners. The profits were enormous. The laws were not enforced, and the slave population increased rapidly.

The purchase of the Louisiana Territory (1803), the gaining of Florida by treaty (1819), and the annexation of Texas (1845) all added to the nation's slave population and to the area where slavery had been legalized.

Some white Americans opposed slavery because they thought it was evil and a denial of every noble statement in both the Constitution and the Declaration of Independence. Others considered it a constant threat and a heavy burden. As a threat they considered the ultimate possibility of slave uprisings. As a burden slave labor without pay handicapped white workers who wanted decent wages for their services.

Thomas Jefferson, principal author of the Declaration of Independence and president from 1801 to 1809, owned slaves. However, he wrote in his memoirs: "Nothing is more certainly written in the book of fate, than these people are to be free. My countrymen! It is written in a better volume than the book of fate: It is written in the laws of Nature and of Nature's God."

Owners used every method they could think of to prevent their slaves from running away. The masters watched them closely, and they had certain favored slaves to spy on the others. A "good" slave received small favors for reporting on the "bad" ones. Extra food,

NEGROES.

Sale of Negroes.

On the 1st of October next my house will be opened and a large supply of all classes of Negroes offered for sale, imported from Virginia, Maryland and Georgia. Afterwards, during the whole season, the supply shall be kept good by the receipt of large lots of the choicest Negroes to be had from the above States. Apply at 54 Baronne street, between Common and Gravier, and two squares west of the St. Charles Hotel. [o6 59—9m¶] WALTER L. CAMPBELL.

Just Received.

Forty very likely young NEGROES, consisting of Field Hands, Mechanics, Seamstresses, House Servants, &c., and for sale, for cash or good city paper. Apply to C. F. HATCHER,
o19—tf 195 Gravier street, New Orleans.

Negroes for Sale.

Having removed from Esplanade to the corner of Baronne and Gravier streets, two squares west of the St. Charles Hotel, where I will keep constantly on hand a choice lot of Maryland and Virginia Negroes, consisting of Field Hands, House Servants, Mechanics, Cooks, Washers and Ironers, Seamstresses, &c.; all of which will be sold low for cash, or on time for good city acceptances.
n8 59—6m ¶ J. M. WILSON.

Carolina and Virginia Negroes for Sale.

I have received Fifty Carolina and Virginia Negroes, consisting of Field Hands, Cooks, Washers and Ironers; also, two No. 1 Blacksmiths, one No. 1 Bricklayer, five good Carpenters, and one good Cooper. Will be receiving fresh gangs every month during the season, which I will sell low for cash, or good 12 months' city acceptance. Persons wishing to purchase would do well to give me a call before purchasing elsewhere. Apply to
H. F. PETERSON, 15 Perdido street,
o24—6m¶ between St. Charles and Carondelet.

C. F. Hatcher,

No. 195 Gravier street, New Orleans, La.—Liberal Advances made on Property placed in my hands for Sale—Slaves—Texas, Mississippi and Louisiana Lands Bought and Sold.
C. M. JOHNSON, Superintendent Slave Depot. NOTICE TO MERCHANTS, PLANTERS, TRADERS and Owners of Slaves—Having made extensive alterations and accommodations on my old stand, I am now prepared to receive and accommodate from two to three hundred slaves, for sale on commission. I can also accommodate the owners with good board and comfortable rooms, on reasonable terms. Those having business in my line would do well to call and see for themselves before looking elsewhere, as the inducements I offer are unequaled. A good stock of Negroes for sale will be constantly kept on hand, consisting of Field Hands, Mechanics, House Servants, Seamstresses, Nurses, Hair Dressers, &c. C. F. HATCHER.
New Orleans. September 26, 1859. s23 59—1y

R. H. Elam,

(Formerly of Natchez, Mississippi.)
Has located at No. 58 Baronne and 176 Gravier street, New Orleans, two squares in the rear of St. Charles Hotel, where he now has a large lot of SLAVES for sale, which will be regularly recruited by fresh importations during the season.
It is only necessary for my old customers to know where to find me. To others I would say, please give me a trial. o14—6m

For Sale.

Just arrived, with a choice lot of VIRGINIA and CAROLINA NEGROES, consisting of Plantation hands, Blacksmiths, Carpenters, Cooks, Washers, Ironers and Seamstresses, and will be receiving fresh supplies during the season, which I offer for sale, for cash or approved paper. I have removed my office from Esplanade to 90 Baronne street, between Union and Perdido streets, two blocks west of St. Charles Hotel. No brokerage paid on the sale of negroes.
JOHN B. SMITH,
90 Baronne stre t,
a21—8m d & W New Orlean La.

Negroes for Sale.

Just arrived, with 100 Negroes, from Virginia, consisting of Field Hands, House Servants, and Mechanics; and will be receiving fresh lots every month. All of which are offered on accommodating terms at my old stand, corner of Esplanade and Chartres streets, near the Mint. Omnibuses running on Royal and Chartres streets all pass my house.
o5—6m d & W ¶ JOSEPH BRUIN.

Committed,

To the Jail of Greene County, Ala., on the 30th day of June, 1859, a negro man named JIM, who says he belongs to John Studman, who lives in the fork of Red and Black Rivers, and says his master's shipping point is Clark's Depot or Landing on Red River. Said boy is about 30 or 35 years old, weighs about 175 or 180 pounds, 6 feet 1½ inches high, scar on his right wrist, which produced a little stiffness in the little finger of the same hand; color black; full beard.
The owner is hereby notified to come forward, prove property, pay charges and take him away, or he will be dealt with as the law directs.
W. R. HARDAWAY, Sheriff.
Eutaw, July 1, 1859. a24—6m

Slaves for Sale.

I have received near one hundred Negroes on consignment, of all classes—several likely families, which I wish to sell, cheap for cash, or its equivalent. In addition to the above I have since received fifty more Negroes—two of which are first rate Blacksmiths. C. M. RUTHERFORD,
o9—3m No. 68 Baronne street.

Slaves for Sale.

Having permanently established myself in this city, I shall keep constantly on hand a full supply of Negroes, selected for this market, comprising Mechanics and House Servants of every description, and choice Field Hands. My stock already purchased is large, and will be added to as required during the season. Will be sold low for cash or approved city acceptances. A. WIESEMANN,
o3—3m 177 Gravier street.

MEDICAL CARDS.

The Chief Attributes of Manhood

ARE frequently lost or suspended by malpractice and vicious habits; they can be infallibly restored to a natural tone by "TRIESEMAR, 1, 2 or 3." Full details in the book "Human Frailty, or Physiological Researches," by Dr. BARROW, 194 Bleeker street, New York. Price 25 cents. Sent free everywhere.
Sold also by J. WRIGHT & CO.,
d9 - 1m Chartres street, N. O.

For Gonorrhea, Gleet, Pains in the Back

and all Urinary Affections.
NO Preparation can compare with the celebrated European Remedy SPECIFIC SOLUTION. It is purely vegetable, of pleasant flavor, and is guaranteed. Among Physicians it is popular, and its reputation is world-wide.
Sole Agent for the United States,
B. ABRAMS, Druggist,
n19 59—1y 44 Camp st., opposite Canal Bank,
New Orleans.

Old Established Dispensary of Dr. James,

82 Customhouse street, (Old Number.)
Between Royal and Bourbon streets, New Orleans.
CURES Scrofula, Syphilis, Mercurial Diseases, Rheumatism, Nervous and General Debility, Impotence, Seminal Weakness, &c.
Diseases peculiar to Females, such as Amenorrhea, constitutional and sympathetic; Dysmenorrhea, idiopathic and symptomatic; Metrorrhagia, essential, sympathetic and symptomatic; Chlorosis, &c.
All of the above maladies are speedily and effectually cured, and without mercurial drugs or other poisonous compounds.
Remember, Dr. JAMES'S DISPENSARY is 82 (old number) Customhouse street, between Royal and Bourbon streets, New Orleans, La.
Separate rooms for patients.
Consultations private and confidential.
Hours of attendance, from 8 A. M. to 8 P. M.
n2—tje2*

a better place to sleep, an easier job—these were some of the enticements slaves received.

But the strongest hold the master had on his slaves was fear. Slaves feared being beaten, being starved, or being killed. In slavery the brutality of master or keeper was necessary. Owners knew that if blacks were treated as normal human beings, they would refuse to submit. The owners and their hired managers, or overseers, kept their slaves in fear.

Beating was the usual punishment. Slaves were beaten with whips and with clubs. It was common practice to select a favored slave to do the beating. This practice had double value for the owner. First, it relieved the master from an onerous task. Second, it helped to keep slaves from uniting under the leadership of one of their own. Masters deliberately promoted distrust among the blacks.

Beating was a common form of punishment inflicted on slaves who were not properly submissive to their owners.

Yet, in spite of the complex means of keeping slaves in fear, many did escape. Also, some revolted and killed their masters. Those who revolted were usually killed before they made good their strike for freedom. Although many failed in their attempts to escape, others—thousands of them—fled to the North.

Most of them crowded into the cities, working at their trades, organizing to help others coming behind them, all the while trying to work themselves into the mainstream of American life. They wanted to show that they could be first-class citizens in the United States of America.

John Brown saw some of the free blacks who had escaped to the North. He knew they were badly treated. They were not considered citizens, even though some had fought for American freedom in the Revolutionary War and again in the War of 1812. They were between slavery and freedom.

John Brown was not well, and he was entirely without funds when he returned to Ohio from Pennsylvania in 1835. He was not, however, without hopes and a strong desire to succeed in business. With borrowed money he speculated in land, developed a plan to build a canal, and organized a cattle company. He made cattle drives overland into Connecticut. He visited Boston and established a plan to supply the New England Wool Company with raw material from Ohio.

After each of these ventures he found himself deeper and deeper in debt.

During this period he was more and more immersed in antislavery activities. On his trips east he read the many publications and he saw reactions to the issue of slavery. In Ohio antislavery societies were being organized as well as proslavery forces. Laws kept some ten thousand free Ohio blacks in a status of less than citizenship. To live in the state a free black man had to be bonded by two white men. Blacks could not vote. Their children could not attend school, although blacks paid school taxes. They were constantly under suspicion. Escaped slaves were seized, and those who protected them were punished.

In 1837 Elijah Lovejoy, an antislavery newspaper publisher, was killed by a proslavery mob in Alton, Illinois. At a protest meeting in Hudson, Ohio, John Brown rose and lifting his right hand said, "Here before God, in the presence of these witnesses, from this time, I consecrate my life to the destruction of slavery."

Many of the people of Ohio were opposed to slavery. A few of them worked to have the whole system abolished everywhere. They were the abolitionists. The free blacks who lived in the North were often involved in helping others to become free.

To the south of Ohio were Virginia (now West Virginia) and Kentucky. In both of these states slaveholding and slave trading were legal. The Ohio River was the boundary between slave territory in the South and free territory in the North. To the north of Ohio lay Canada, a place of refuge for ex-slaves.

Through Ohio black men and women traveled, singly and in pairs and in groups. They moved mostly at night. They hid by day. Many of them traveled by the "Underground Railroad." This was a system for helping escaping slaves. Experienced "conductors," usually black men or women, led them. Often the conductors got them across the Ohio River in boats borrowed from helping persons who lived on the banks of the river. The conductors knew farmers and other citizens who would shelter the runaways in their homes. Such stopping places were called "stations." Those who provided the hideaways were "stationmasters."

John Brown was a stationmaster. John Brown Jr. remembered seeing when he was about five years old his father help runaway slaves. In the night a black man and his wife came to the house. Someone had told the slaves that they would be safe there. John Brown received them. He fed them and talked gently to them. They knew they were in danger, and they were afraid.

While Brown was making a place for them to sleep, they heard the sound of horses. Brown rushed them out the back door and hid them in a swampy place. He gave them arms and told them to defend themselves if men came to capture them.

When he knew that the danger had passed, Brown went again and brought the fugitives back to the house. Later he sent them on their way, northward.

His daughter Ruth wrote that her father at one time had some "very respectable Negroes" working for him on the farm. One Sunday these people, with some of their black friends, went to church. Members of the congregation seated them in the far back and behind a stove. John Brown, very indignant, had the black people move forward to occupy his family pew. Members of the Brown family went to the back to take seats behind the stove.

"The whole church were down on him," she wrote.

"The minister looked angry, but I remember my father's determined look. . . . My brothers were so disgusted to see such a mockery of religion that they left the church and have never belonged to another."

Her brother John Jr. also told the story. He added that John Brown made a speech to the church, and that shortly thereafter the deacons canceled his membership.

The children of John Brown came to share their father's hatred of slavery and his compassion for victims of the system.

John Jr. later wrote about one time when his father called his children about him. He talked to them about the evils of holding men as property, of the brutalizing effects on the owners as well as on the enslaved. He told them about his own determination to make war on slavery. His older sons entered a solemn compact to join him in this war.

Ruth said that her father was very kind and gentle most of the time, but that he was also very strict.

> Whenever he and I were alone, he never failed to give me the best of advice . . . He always seemed interested in my work, and would come around and look at it when I was sewing or knitting; and when I was learning to spin he always praised me if he saw I was improving. He used to say: "Try to do whatever you do in the very best possible manner."
>
> When his children were ill with scarlet fever, he took care of us himself. . . . When any of the family were sick he did not often trust watchers to care for the sick one, but sat up himself and was like a tender mother. At one time he sat up every night for two weeks while mother was sick, for fear he would over-

sleep if he went to bed, and then the fire would go out and she take cold.

She also said, "He used to whip me often for telling lies."

Brown lived simply. He worked hard. He never used tobacco, wine, or liquor of any kind; and for some reason which none of his children seem to have explained, he did not use cheese or butter. About his studying, Ruth wrote:

> My dear father's favorite books on a historical character were Rollin's Ancient History, Josephus, Plutarch, the Lives of Napoleon and His Marshals, and the Life of Oliver Cromwell . . . but above all others the Bible was his favorite volume and he had such perfect knowledge of it that when any person was reading it he would correct the least mistake. . . . When he would come home at night, tired out with labor, he would before going to bed, ask some of the family to read chapters and would almost always say, "Read one of David's Psalms."
>
> He was a great admirer of Oliver Cromwell. Of Colored heroes, Nat Turner, and Cinques, stood first in his esteem. How often have I heard him speak in admiration of Cinques' character and management.

Perhaps some of the children had their questions, but if they did have doubts, they did not show them. Most of them believed in their father. They were determined to be with him in the consecration of his life.

They shared his life, and in the end some of them were to share his death.

4

Brown Reveals His Plan

In all his activities, in his business affairs and in his travels, Brown was always seeking ways to attack the practice of slavery. He believed that he might help slaves take action for themselves, and he felt that ex-slaves, now free, could do a great deal. He realized that the conditions of slavery had not contributed to the ability of these people to live in a free society. They had not learned to read, to use money, to plan. In slavery they had lived on a bare subsistence level. Even as free men their existence was perilous. They existed in danger of being attacked, of having their possessions taken from them, even of being seized and rushed southward back into slavery. They could not hope that the law would provide protection.

Brown's business activities took him away from Ohio. His observations helped him develop a plan for the destruction of slavery.

Owen Brown, the father of John Brown, had prospered in his business of tanning, and he had expanded his farming. People respected the elder Mr. Brown as a community leader. He was appointed a member of the board of trustees of Oberlin College when it was founded in 1839. This college was set up by antislavery people. From its beginning it provided education for black youths as well as white.

From his father John Brown learned that the wealthy landowner Gerrit Smith, a resident of Peterboro, New York, supported the college's position and had given to the college certain Virginia lands. However, title was clouded. Boundaries were not clearly defined, and squatters had taken over choice sections.

Early in 1840 Brown wrote to the trustees proposing to survey the land and define its boundaries. He would undertake this mission at minimum cost if he would be allowed to purchase some of the land on reasonable terms. He said he wanted to establish a home for his family, and he spoke of providing school facilities for whites and blacks. This had been his hope for a long time.

The trustees happily agreed. Brown set out immediately. He liked what he saw. He admired the country, the land, and the people he met. By the summer he had accomplished his task. He sent his report to Oberlin and described the site he had chosen for himself. The trustees were pleased. They authorized transfer of one thousand acres of land to "Brother John Brown of Hudson."

He was offered the land in good faith, but he delayed, and the Oberlin offer was withdrawn.

Later, in 1844, he entered an arrangement with Simon

Perkins, a wealthy businessman of Akron, Ohio. Perkins owned a large sheep farm west of the town. Brown moved his family to a plain farmhouse on this land. With help from his sons and some sheep dogs, it seemed that Brown would at last overcome financial difficulties. He had a good knowledge of wool. He contributed articles on the subject to the *Ohio Cultivator* and to other journals.

It was not long before Brown emerged as a spokesman for western farmers who claimed that eastern dealers were cheating them by keeping prices low and by dishonestly grading the fleece so that they could purchase fine and medium grades at low-grade prices. Brown persuaded Simon Perkins that he could handle the situation and at the same time make money for themselves and other Ohio and Pennsylvania wool growers. In June the two men set up a partnership as Perkins and Brown, with a warehouse in Springfield, Massachusetts, on the bank of the Connecticut River. He moved his family again and set up housekeeping in a simple house near the warehouse. Brown worked hard at the business, and his son Jason helped with bookkeeping and letter writing. However, the business did not make profits.

Some people feel that John Brown did not succeed in business because he gave so much time and thought to the cause of liberty. Wherever he went he was interested in the black people he saw, and he was always considering the plight of those who were enslaved.

It was in Springfield that Brown first became well acquainted with blacks. He met with them as individuals, and he hired some in his business. He visited in their homes and got to know them as families. He went to their churches, and he often sat quietly in their meetings while they talked about their problems and their hopes and their fears. With them he considered himself an equal. They sat at his table, and he sat at theirs.

He saw free men asserting themselves as individuals and in groups. He took time to visit other cities to meet more.

In Boston he met Dr. John V. DeGrasse, who had studied medicine in the United States and in France and was a respected member of the Massachusetts Medical Society, and Attorney Robert Morris, who was a member of the bar association. In the same city the ex-slave William Wells Brown was writing his second book, *Clotel*, which was later published in England. It was a novel subtitled *The President's Daughter*.

In Philadelphia some free men had prospered in business. Stephen Smith was a successful lumber merchant, and James Forten had a business in the making of sails; William Still, in addition to his business as a coal dealer, was an organizer in the Underground Railroad system.

Every city in the North had organizations such as the League of Freedom, Liberty League, American Mysteries. Even in Canada, a group called the "True Bands" had several hundred members in each of fourteen bands.

In 1847 John Brown made his first contact with Frederick Douglass, a man who was to be his friend for the rest of his life, the first man to whom Brown outlined his Master Plan.

Brown had heard about Frederick Douglass. He had read *The North Star*, which Douglass published, as well as William Lloyd Garrison's paper *The Liberator*. He did not endorse Garrison's nonviolent approach. Brown liked the forceful statements of Douglass. He invited Douglass to visit him at his Springfield home.

Frederick Douglass was an ex-slave. While he was a boy in Maryland, a kind mistress helped him learn to read. After that he studied, worked hard, plotted, failed in a first attempt to escape, and finally at the age of twenty-one successfully made the trip from Baltimore to New York and found friends who were in the work of the Underground Railroad.

Douglass became active in the abolition movement. Leaders in antislavery societies found him to be a good speaker who vividly described the evils of slavery and readily bared his back to show the marks of brutal beatings. He wrote as well as he spoke. In 1845 he started

Frederick Douglass

publishing his own paper, *The North Star.* The name suggested the guiding star that runaways had to keep before them as they traveled through the country at night.

The two men first met at Brown's office. Douglass was impressed; the office and warehouse was in a large brick building on a busy street. He was disappointed, however, when he saw the simple, scantily furnished home in which Brown lived with his family. Yet, Douglass found himself welcome, and he saw that the family was happy. There were no servants. The mother and the daughters and sons did all the serving.

Douglass later wrote in detail about this visit. He described John Brown as being lean, strong, and sinewy, built for times of trouble and fitted to grapple with hardships. Under six feet tall, less than 150 pounds in weight, about 50 years old, he presented a figure straight and symmetrical as a mountain pine. His head was not large, but compact and high. His hair was coarse and slightly gray. His face was smooth-shaved. He had a strong, square mouth and a broad, prominent chin. He moved with long, springing, race-horse steps, neither seeking nor shunning observation.

After a simple meal of soup, cabbages, and potatoes served on a clean scrubbed table without a cloth, Brown led to the subject of slavery, denouncing the system and saying that slaves had full rights to seek their liberty in any way they could (by any means necessary) and that slaveholders had forfeited their right to live. He said that neither moral persuasion nor political action could ever abolish the system.

Then, according to Douglass, Brown said that he had been looking for some black men to whom he could reveal his plan. It was not to create a general uprising with the killing of the slave masters. Yet he was not entirely against the shedding of blood. He wanted to see slaves fight for their freedom. He wanted only to help them.

Pointing to a map with the Allegheny range stretching from New York into the southern states, Brown said, "These mountains are the basis of my plan. . . . God placed them there for the emancipation of the Negro race. They are full of natural forts where one man in defense will be equal to a hundred for attack. . . .

"My plan, then, is to take about twenty-five picked men and . . . post them in squads of fives. The most persuasive of these shall go down to the fields from time to time and induce the slaves to join them."

He thought he could gather a body of a hundred men who would be moving the slaves out in increasing numbers. The bravest and strongest of the slaves would join his force. Others could be sent north by the Underground Railroad.

Douglass protested that slave owners would only strengthen their own protection, and they would fight.

"They would employ bloodhounds," he said, "to hunt you out of the mountains."

"They might attempt it," Brown replied, "but . . . we should whip them." He added that if the worst came, he would only be killed, and he had no better use for his life than to lay it down in the cause of the slave.

Friendship between the two men continued for the remainder of John Brown's life.

5

Establishing a Home at North Elba

Brown saw in a project of Gerrit Smith's the means of advancing his cause. Smith, who had given land to Oberlin College, had also set aside 120,000 acres in the Adirondack Mountains in northeastern New York for families of black people. A few families had accepted the offer of help. They had settled in a community called North Elba, but the winters were hard and cold. Most of the land was not highly productive, and the blacks were not skilled in farming. White settlers and dishonest surveyors united to push the blacks off the better lands.

John Brown—farmer, stockman, surveyor—went to see Smith.

"I see by the papers," he said, "that you have offered land to colored men on the condition that they cultivate it. Now they are most inexperienced in this kind of work, and unused to the climate, while I am familiar with both." He then offered his help. It was in the form of a proposal. "If you will give me land I will clear it, and plant it, showing the Negroes how such work should be done. I will also employ some of them on my land and will look after them in all ways, and will be a kind of father to them."

Gerrit Smith had never seen John Brown before. He must have recognized the sincerity of this great, gaunt, powerful-looking person with the steel-gray eyes. He must have seen in him strong character as well as great sympathy. Mr. Smith accepted the proposal, gave Brown 244 acres of land at a nominal price of one dollar per acre, and promised to help in other ways.

After a visit to the area Brown arranged to move his family to the North Elba tract. John Jr. and Jason had married and established themselves with their families in Ohio. They did not wish to move. At North Elba, Brown's daughter Ruth met young Henry Thompson, whose parents had a farm there. He was already a dedicated opponent of slavery. He and Ruth were married, and he took charge of building the house for the family of his bride. Brown's wife, Mary, was sick much of the time. She continued to bear children, but Ruth shared the housekeeping responsibilities.

In an effort to salvage the wool business, Brown had 200,000 pounds of his prime fleece shipped to England, and he went to London where he tried to sell it in competition with Scottish and English wool. He was unable to sell at a profit. He and his backers lost money, but Brown took advantage of further opportunities to work on his plan.

He met some of the people in Europe who were active in their own antislavery movement. He told them that he held a commission direct from God to act against slavery, and he disclosed something of his Master Plan. It is not recorded that he received encouragement.

He did, however, study about the science of war. He read history and visited battle sites and examined forts and arrangements for defense.

At home, the firm of Perkins and Brown went out of business. Brown was sued by some who claimed they had been defrauded. He lost in several suits, but he had nothing with which to pay the judgments. Simon Perkins lost about $40,000 in the venture, but he maintained his confidence in Brown. Perkins tried to persuade Brown to return to Ohio and continue in the business of sheep and wool.

Brown was involved in the project at North Elba, and he would not go back. His wife, Mary, and ten children were installed there. They were quite as comfortable as in any situation they had known.

In 1850 John Brown was trying to settle his affairs in Springfield and at the same time get established at North Elba. All the while he was active with abolitionists. His special interest was with the leaders who were black. Henry Highland Garnet, a well-educated man, was one of these. Two black women, Harriet Tubman, an ex-slave who was an Underground Railroad conductor, and Sojourner Truth, another ex-slave, a speaker and organizer, were among his friends. At North Elba he worked to help families of free blacks. Visitors were shocked to see that he treated these people with respect.

One visitor was Richard Henry Dana, the author of *Two Years Before the Mast*. Dana wrote that he found Brown a strong abolitionist and "some kind of king" in the community. He was annoyed to observe that

Brown referred to black neighbors as "Mister" and let them eat at the same table with his family.

In the year 1850 a new fugitive slave law gave slave owners or their representatives the right to capture escaped slaves wherever they might be found. Slave catchers sought for escapees, many of whom were living as free men and women, mixing with blacks who were legally free. Slave catchers also seized blacks who were not runaways. The slavers would destroy the identification certificates, or "free papers," that free blacks had to carry. Then they would hustle their captives southward and sell them as slaves.

In the year 1850 a new law gave slave owners
the right to capture fugitive slaves wherever they were found.
Slave catchers also seized blacks who were not runaways.

Brown saw black people living in terror. Abolitionists were angered. Protest meetings were held.

Brown said in North Elba and in Springfield to his black friends, "You must not take this evil lying down. Organize. . . . Form guerrilla bands. . . . Fight this wicked law with the sword."

In North Elba members of the Brown family swore they would protect their friends even if it meant imprisonment or death. Ruth said of their faithful boy, Cyrus, a runaway, "We would all have defended him though the womenfolk had resorted to hot water."

In Springfield Brown organized the United States League of the Gileadites. This was a militant band of forty-four men and women who pledged to fight to defend themselves and other blacks.

Brown gave them certain precepts:

> Be firm, detached, and cool;
> Stand by one another and by your friends while a drop
>   of blood remains;
> Be hanged if you must, but tell no tales out of school;
> Do not delay one moment after you are ready;
> Let the first blow be the sign for all to engage;
> When you engage your enemies, make clean work of
>   it.

He tried to make them know that "the trial for life of one bold and somewhat successful man, for defending his rights in good earnest, would arouse more sympathy throughout the nation than the suffering of all the slaves."

For the next several years, although he did not spend

A meeting of the Gileadites at Springfield, Massachusetts.

much time there, Brown considered North Elba his
home. He said that everything there reminded him of
Omnipotence, the quality of being unlimited in power,
ability, or authority. Simon Perkins, in spite of losses,
continued to work with Brown in the area of Akron,

Ohio. Brown managed some of the farmlands belonging to Perkins, and he lived on the Perkins property. Brown's wife, Mary, was not well, and his son Frederick was sickly, suffering from chronic, painful headaches. The young man was considered wild and flighty. Brown let him spend most of his time in the fields watching the sheep.

But Perkins could not agree with Brown about slavery. Perkins considered Brown impulsive and uncompromising, which indeed he was.

Brown worked hard and faithfully in the fields, but he was making trips to attend meetings and conferences. He was especially agitated by continuing acts of Congress and government officials in Washington that encouraged the spread of slavery in the West. The Kansas-Nebraska Act (1854) was one of these.

In 1854 he finally broke with Perkins. But he had no money to return to North Elba. On rented land in Ohio he was determined to become independent by farming and raising sheep. His wife became pregnant again. Frederick almost died following an operation and finally made a satisfactory recovery.

Ruth and her husband, Henry Thompson, remained at North Elba. A year after his break with Perkins, John Brown returned to North Elba with his wife and younger children. This was the last time he moved the family.

6

War in Kansas

In 1820 an act of Congress known as the Missouri Compromise ruled that slavery should be permitted in Missouri, which had applied for statehood. The same act declared that other territories to be admitted at later dates should not be slaveholding. Maine, which was admitted to the Union in 1820, was a free state. Thus, by allowing slavery in Missouri, Congress was able to maintain the balance between free and slave states.

This compromise displeased antislavery people in the northern states where slavery was prohibited. It also displeased proslavery people in the southern states where slavery was the basis of the economy. People in the South felt that their interest lay in the development of slavery. It was increasingly referred to as the "peculiar institution."

Now Kansas was the territory just west of the state of Missouri. Its land and climate were similar to that of Missouri. Its soil was equally rich. Slaveholders in

Missouri looked to Kansas and felt that this, too, should be slave territory.

By 1850 the population of Kansas had grown to between 8,000 and 9,000, including perhaps 200 slaves. In the next few years many settlers from slave states went to Kansas, taking their slaves with them. Slave owners were determined to make Kansas another slave state. During the same period, a large number of persons from the North went out because they were interested in colonizing or filling up the state with those who were opposed to slavery. Northern newspapers carried glowing accounts about the wonders of Kansas. It was referred to as the great wide-open space, the new frontier, the place for settlers who were interested in making homes. Land was free and the sky was bright and blue. Every opportunity for freedom and development was there.

And so it was that in October of 1854, five of John Brown's sons—John Jr., Jason, Owen, Frederick, and Salmon, then residents of the state of Ohio—made their plans to go west. Their combined wealth consisted of eleven head of cattle and three horses. Owen, Frederick, and Salmon moved out in the fall of 1854. After wintering in Illinois they traveled with their wagons and cattle and horses to a place in Kansas about ten miles west of the town of Osawatomie. The following spring John Jr. and Jason, with their wives and children, set out by the water route, going down the Ohio River and up the Mississippi to St. Louis. There they purchased supplies, including tents, a plow, a hand-operated mill for grinding corn, and other implements and tools. They were warned of trouble ahead. A friendly Virginian told John Jr. that proslavery people had organized "Annoy-

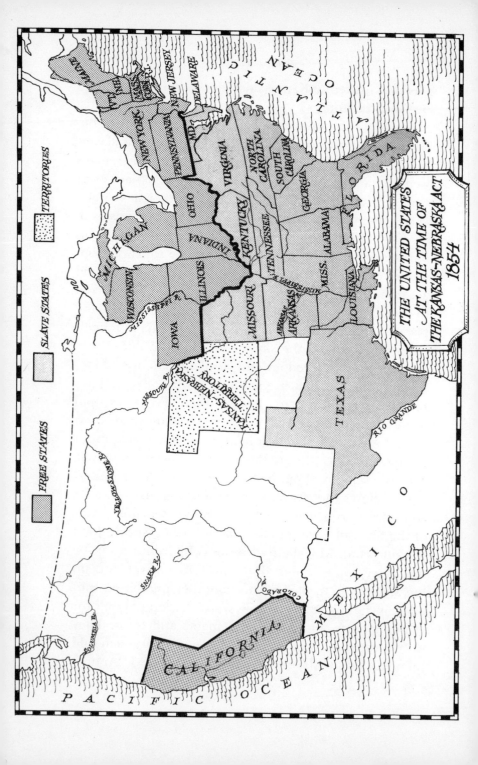

ance Associations" to scare antislavery settlers away. At St. Louis they boarded the steamer *New Lucy* to travel up the Missouri River.

John Jr. wrote his own account of their trip:

> We chose the river route, taking passage on the steamer, *New Lucy* which too late we found crowded with passengers, mostly men from the South bound for Kansas. That they were from the South was plainly indicated by their language and dress; while their drinking, profanity, and display of revolvers and bowie-knives openly worn as an essential part of their make-up—clearly showed the class to which they belonged, and that their mission was to aid in establishing slavery in Kansas.
>
> A box of fruit trees and grape-vines which my brother Jason had brought from Ohio, our plough, and the few agricultural implements we had on the deck of the steamer looked lonesome; for these were all we could see which were adapted to the occupations of peace. Then for the first time arose in our minds the query: Must the fertile prairies of Kansas, through a struggle at arms, be first secured to freedom before free men can sow and reap? If so, how poorly we were prepared for such work will be seen when I say that, for arms, five of us brothers had only two small squirrel rifles and one revolver. But before we reached our destination, other matters claimed our attention. Cholera, which then prevailed to some extent at St. Louis, broke out among our passengers, a number of whom died. Among them brother Jason's son, Austin, aged four years, the elder of his two children, fell a victim to this scourge; and while our boat lay by for repair of a broken rudder at Waverly, Mo., we buried him at

night near the panic-stricken town, our lonely way illu-
mined only by the lightning of a furious thunderstorm.
True to his spirit of hatred of Northern people, our
captain, without warning to us on shore, cast off his
lines and left us to make our way by stage to Kansas
City to which place we had already paid our fare by
boat. Before we reached there, however, we became
very hungry, and endeavored to buy food at various
farm houses on the way; but the occupants, judging
from our speech that we were not from the south, always denied us, saying, "We have nothing for you."

John Jr. described how the slave owners from Missouri
came over to Kansas by force and attacked those who
were against slavery. Homes were burned. Cattle were
driven off. Many people were badly injured, and some
were killed. His brothers also wrote to their father. They
told him about the conditions in Kansas, and they reaf-
firmed their determination to help make Kansas free
territory. They asked him to send help, particularly guns
and ammunition.

In the East John Brown was developing his plans.
He had already fixed his eye on Harpers Ferry. He well
knew the Allegheny Mountains and the valleys running
north and south between the mountain ridges. The valleys were lines of the Underground Railroad. Harriet
Tubman and others moved along these routes with escaping slaves. John Brown's farm was at North Elba,
at the northern extremity of the Alleghenies. Harpers
Ferry was straight south, in slaveholding Virginia, just
beyond the line of Pennsylvania, where slavery was prohibited.

It is about sixty miles from the capital at Washington,

D.C. There the Shenandoah River from the west flows into the Potomac River flowing south. The town is at the bottom of the "V" which the rivers form. In the town was an armory, a storehouse for weapons, and a factory for making rifles. The place was poorly defended. No soldiers were stationed there. To seize this storehouse with its rich prize of guns and ammunition was an important factor in Brown's Master Plan. Certainly he would not have halted his planning or changed his course without careful consideration.

So he did consider it carefully.

He attended a convention in Syracuse, New York, where hundreds of abolitionists gathered to discuss the antislavery movement. This convention was a revelation to John Brown. He found that he was by no means alone and that in the movement were persons of great means, among them his friend Gerrit Smith. There were others who were able and willing to contribute money to Brown's cause.

At the convention Brown made a fiery speech. He announced that he already had sons in Kansas and that he had others who were ready to go. He said that he was willing to go to them and help them defend themselves and help them build up the population of antislavery people in that territory. He explained that he was not a man of means. Alone he could not provide adequately.

He read the letter from John Jr., and he said that the invasion of Kansas by a proslavery army of killers was a greater evil than the action of slave catchers searching for runaways in the northern cities.

Both Frederick Douglass and Gerrit Smith spoke in

support of Brown. They were able to raise some money to help him.

He wrote to his wife, "The convention has been one of the most interesting meetings I ever attended in my life; and I made a great addition to the number of warm and honest friends."

Brown left for Kansas that summer, taking with him his son-in-law Henry Thompson, husband of his daughter Ruth. Another son, Oliver, who was working in Chicago, joined Brown and Henry Thompson as they went through Illinois. Daughter Ruth, wife Mary, twenty-year-old son Watson, and the younger children remained on the farm at North Elba.

Ruth wrote that as her father left them he said, "If it is so painful for us to part with the hope of meeting again, how dreadful must be the feelings of hundreds of poor slaves who are separated for life."

The party traveled with a horse and covered wagon loaded with cured pork, beans, flour, and meal, also guns and swords, gunpowder and caps. The guns and ammunition were concealed under Brown's surveying instruments.

Guided by a diagram, or map, which John Jr. had sent to North Elba, John Brown arrived at "Brown's Station" in the fall of 1855. He found members of the family weak and demoralized. All of them, except two of the children, were sick with the ague. They were living in makeshift tents, and as he wrote to the others in North Elba, they were "shivering over their little fires all exposed to the dreadfully cutting winds."

Jason had been depressed since the death of his son

in Missouri. His wife, Ellen, was anxious to return to the comparative comfort of Ohio.

"It's the people," Ellen said. "The people who own slaves and want to make Kansas a slave state. They hate us, treat us like dirt under their feet. They call us 'jay-hawks.' "

"Jayhawks?" Brown asked. "What's the meaning of that?"

Jason explained.

"It's something they lay on us because we're poor. They say we're raggedy as jaybirds and hungry as hawks. I don't care, myself, but Ellen and the womenfolk take it hard."

"Jayhawks, eh!" Brown answered with his right hand raised high. "Raggedy and hungry, maybe, but we are instruments in the hand of an almighty God. They can call us jayhawks but we'll show them that the jayhawks are under God's command in His war against the sin of slavery."

Just at that time the proslavery people were not active. This was only because of the inclement weather. The Browns and all other antislavery people had been continuously harassed and more than harassed: they had been attacked. Some had been beaten. Homes had been burned. Crops had been ruined. Livestock had been stolen.

As his wagon was unloaded John Brown lifted out what he considered the most precious of his cargo. It was the body of four-year-old Austin, who had died of cholera. Brown had stopped in the settlement at Waverly, Missouri, to disinter the child's body. Now they dug a new grave and laid it away in the burying ground of Brown's Station. It was the first of several.

John Brown's thoughtful act lifted some of Jason's depression, and his wife agreed to remain in Kansas.

Brown soon learned that the people who sought freedom for the slaves outnumbered those who wanted to legalize slavery. The New England Emigrant Aid Society was one of the organizations that backed settlers from the North. They had believed that the issue would be settled by voting. Those from the slave states were not depending on votes. They had decided to maintain their will by force and physical power. They were determined to control the lawmakers and the lawmaking processes.

One of the leaders of the proslavery forces, General Benjamin Franklin Stringfellow of Missouri, said, "To those who have qualms of conscience as to violating laws, state or national, the time has come when such impositions must be disregarded, as your right and property are endangered."

Five thousand Missourians had crossed into the Kansas territory and voted. They elected a legislature and a congressional delegate. Their government was set up with Lawrence, Kansas, as the capital. By 1855 they were very strong, and they established laws which definitely defended the institution of slavery. One of their laws made it a felony even to make a statement against the right of slaveholding.

On October 2, 1855, the *Cleveland Morning Leader* carried a story from Leavenworth, Kansas. It opened with the statement, "Murder rules in Kansas."

It continued with a detailed report of an election day when Missouri proslavery men crossed into Kansas in armed bands: "They rushed in a drunken and riotous frenzy to the extreme of barbarity, and capped the climax of their atrocities by murder."

Settlers in Kansas who wanted the slave trade forbidden were called "free-staters." They recognized the threat of the proslavery forces of Kansas supported by uncontrolled mobs from Missouri.

Free-staters found themselves in three groups. The first hated slavery for moral reasons. A second group hated blacks because they were not white. A third group hated slaves because slaves were providing free labor for the owners. At one time it seemed that these divergent hatreds would weaken the strength of the free-staters. However, in the fall of 1855, at Big Springs, Kansas, they held a convention at which they agreed unanimously on a policy of passive resistance with the threat of active resistance to the illegally elected controlling body. They proceeded to organize a separate territorial government. They made an appeal to Congress and the nation. Topeka was established as their capital.

This meeting took place before the arrival of John Brown, but his sons were present, and they were active in the new organization. Brown was not too late to witness some of the brutalities and to join actively in the fight.

In November of 1855 a peaceful immigrant from New England was murdered by a proslavery settler.

The authorities, instead of arresting the murderer, arrested a friend of the victim, a witness of the killing. Free-staters stormed the jail in Lawrence, the official capital, and released the friend of the murder victim.

This act infuriated the slave-staters. They raised a

company of 1,500 men, most of whom came over from
Missouri. They moved against Lawrence. They knew that
most of the citizens there were free-staters. They did
not attack at that time because a storm came up.
Through the winter bad weather continued to discour-
age action on the part of the mobs. However, with the
coming of spring, the slave-staters were active again.

In the United States Senate it was said that Kansas
had been "won" by the proslavery people. In the month
of February 1856, President Franklin Pierce in an official proclamation denounced the Topeka free-state legislature as an illegal assembly. He confirmed the government's support of proslavery actions. Then he ordered
the federal troops to aid the territorial officers in carry-
ing out the proslavery legislation.

The slave-staters were not satisfied. They knew that
most of the new settlers were free-staters. In May of
1856 they struck.

First the proslavery marshall arrested the leaders of
the free-state movement. Then the mob attacked. Two
thousand Missourians with banners flying fell upon the
city. They killed, they looted, they burned half the city.
Lawrence was left in ruins.

In Washington, Senator Charles Sumner of Massachusetts denounced the attack as a "crime without example
in the history of the past." He said some of his fellow
congressmen were the real murderers of the men of
Lawrence. Two days later Congressman Preston Brooks
from South Carolina saw Sumner writing at his seat.
Brooks came behind Sumner. With his walking stick he
beat the senator into unconsciousness. The news of the
attack on Senator Sumner shocked the North. It person-

alized the indignation of the people of Boston, which was in Sumner's district. At the same time Brooks received from southern admirers a gold-headed cane inscribed, "Use knock-down arguments."

In Kansas the free-staters were overwhelmed. They had not been outvoted legally, but they had seen all controls taken over by the invasion of slaveholders.

John Brown told his sons that the time for active resistance had come. They had been well known as free-staters. The homes of John Jr. and Jason had been attacked. Certain leaders of the slave-staters had vowed to get the settlers at Brown's Station, including "the old man."

On May 24, four days after the sacking of Lawrence, a brutal assault was committed on a free-state man. John P. Doyle, a farmer from Tennessee, and his sons were principals and most active in the attack. Then members of the Doyle family called upon the women of the Brown family and gave warning, saying "Tell your men that if they don't leave right off, we'll come back tomorrow and kill them."

Later the same night John Brown's four sons, his son-in-law, and two others summarily executed five persons. Doyle, the father, and his two sons were the first. A proslavery man known as Dutch Henry was the next. Allen Wilkinson was the fifth man to be slain. One of John Brown's men, Henry Townsend, was also killed. Later John Brown said that he did not take part in this action but he believed the killings were justified and even necessary.

The word went out. John Brown and his sons were hunted men. Warrants of arrest were issued. The old man let it be known that he would not be taken. Word of this act at Osawatomie spread throughout Kansas and the East and South. It focused attention on Kansas and the conflict there, and the name of John Brown was in the center of all the discussion. Among antislavery men in Kansas he was recognized as their leader. He knew something of military tactics. He taught these skills, and he organized bands through Kansas for his followers. Pitched battles were fought. Breastworks and fortifications were thrown up. Women and children organized to feed the fighters and to nurse the wounded.

Proslavery people recruited new help from Missouri and the Deep South. In the East abolitionists became more active. Mass meetings were held in every city, and a great convention met in Buffalo, New York. Money, guns, food, clothes, and more settlers were sent out to Kansas.

John Brown was ever mindful of his Master Plan, which was built around the capture of Harpers Ferry and the movement of runaway slaves from the South to the North. He referred to the plan from time to time, but he found himself too actively engaged in the struggle for a free Kansas to act upon it. As a hunted man, condemned by the existing government, he avoided open contact with people. His sons went on with their house building and farming, but Brown kept to the woods and to the swamps.

He organized a body of thirty-five men who joined him in a solemn oath. They signed a covenant swearing to serve in the free-state cause under John Brown as commander. A set of rules and bylaws was adopted, and military order was enforced. Among the rules was one forbidding the punishment or execution of a prisoner without first giving him a fair and impartial trial. The rules also forbade the use of profane and vulgar talk. Drinking intoxicating beverages or bringing liquor into the camp was considered disorderly.

Brown felt that the battle for Kansas as a free state was being won. He was in several battles. Sons John Jr. and Jason were arrested, imprisoned, and finally released. John Jr. lost his mind and for a short period seemed to be quite helpless.

In the next year attacks on free-staters continued. The homes of John Jr. and Jason were burned down. Both of these sons of John Brown were wounded in the fighting. Henry Thompson, Brown's son-in-law, was also wounded.

On September 7, 1856, Brown wrote more sad news to his family in North Elba:

> On the morning of the 30th of August (1856) an attack was made by the Ruffians on Osawatomie, numbering some four hundred, by whose scouts our dear Frederick was shot dead without warning,—he supposing them to be free-state men, as near as we can learn. One other man, a cousin of Mr. Adair, was murdered about the same time that Frederick was killed, and one badly wounded.
>
> I was about three miles off, where I had some fourteen or fifteen men over night that I had just enlisted to serve under me as regulars. These I collected as well as I could, with some twelve or fifteen more; and in about three-quarters of an hour I attacked them from the wood with thick undergrowth. With this force we threw them in confusion for about fifteen or twenty

An artist's interpretation of John Brown's controversial role in the
violent struggles between slave-staters and free-staters in Kansas.

minutes, during which time we killed or wounded from
seventy to eighty of the enemy,—as they say,—and then
we escaped as well as we could, with one killed while
escaping, two or three wounded, and as many more
missing.

I was struck by a partly spent grape, canister, or rifle
shot, which bruised me some, but did not injure me
seriously. Hitherto the Lord has helped me.

Frederick, the lad who at one time had been fit to
do little more than watch the sheep, was the first of
John Brown's sons to die in the fight for freedom.

We know that the "seventy or eighty of the enemy"

killed or wounded may have been an exaggeration. It was Brown's own story. We know also that the leader of the proslavery fighters reported that he had killed twenty or thirty men, including John Brown. It is not an exaggeration to say that although warrants were issued for his arrest, no one dared approach him. He moved in fierce and righteous anger. People called him "Old Osawatomie" or "Osawatomie Brown." Free-staters believed in him and followed him. Slave-staters hated him—and feared him.

7

Seeking Help for Freedom

Brown's next letter to his wife, dated October 11, 1856, was written from Tabor, Iowa. It said, "I am through Infinite grace, once more in a Free State; and on my way to make you a visit."

With three sons and an escaped slave he started back to the East. Government officers and troops followed. They attempted to overtake the party, and they hoped to make arrests. Brown successfully eluded them although his party was traveling with a covered wagon. His set of surveyor's tools aided in gaining the confidence of people who saw them. They did not think of him as a fighter. Often they supposed him to be a government officer.

In the following years, 1857 and 1858, war activities diminished, but some fighting continued in the southeastern section of Kansas.

Brown did not believe that his work in Kansas was completed. He had referred to his trip as "a visit." For more than a year he sought help from individuals and from organizations in many different states.

"I am trying to raise from twenty to twenty-five thousand dollars," he said, "to enable me to continue my efforts in the cause of freedom. . . . I do not ask for pay, but shall be most grateful for all the assistance I can get."

The strongest organization giving help to free-staters in Kansas was the New England Emigrant Aid Society. Theirs was a program for investment. The leaders expected to receive shares in the settlers' profits. The company failed.

After the burning of Lawrence, Kansas, the National Kansas Committee was formed. Gerrit Smith, previously mentioned, contributed several thousand dollars to the Kansas Committee.

Some older and larger organizations had been working against slavery even before the Kansas struggle developed. Brown knew them and their leaders knew John Brown. Some of them helped him. Others thought he was too radical.

The American Anti-Slavery Society was a large body that was not very aggressive. The members wrote letters, articles, and books. They held meetings and they raised funds, but they abhorred direct action. William Lloyd Garrison was the society's spokesman and leader. He was a good man. He had many friends among the ex-slaves. He tried to win America to the cause of abolition by persuasion. He believed that people could be made to see the evil and the injustice of slavery.

Differing from the position of the American Anti-Slavery Society was the American and Foreign Anti-Slavery Society. Its leadership called for action. England had already abolished slavery. Moral and financial support came to this organization from overseas.

The Free Soil Party, which was primarily political, wanted to abolish slavery by the vote. Its members wanted to elect persons who were opposed to slave traffic. They believed political organization and right voting would bring about the desired ends.

The Liberty Party, also political, believed that voting would help but that action, such as Brown promoted in Kansas, was necessary. Gerrit Smith contributed to the Liberty Party also.

And beyond all of these was the Society of Friends, as the Quakers are called. The Quakers have always been known as a deeply religious people involved in causes that they deem good. They are today active in peace movements. They are in opposition to many of the established rules of government.

A supporter with large amounts of money was George Luther Stearns, a Boston merchant. He and his wife believed in the cause of abolition, and they contributed to the movement.

Richard J. Hinton, an abolitionist who was also a newspaperman and writer, worked very closely with John Brown. He spent time in Kansas. He attended some of the meetings and conventions. He wrote *John Brown and His Men,* a very full account from which much of this information comes. As a matter of fact, Hinton was expected to join John Brown at Harpers Ferry, but for certain reasons John Brown made his move one week earlier than Hinton had expected him to.

Other people were close to John Brown.

Franklin Benjamin Sanborn, a scholar who was identified with the abolition movement, wrote and compiled the *Life and Letters of John Brown, Liberator of Kansas, and Martyr of Virginia.* He was a personal friend and supporter.

Another was James J. Redpath, who was responsible for the publication of John Brown's autobiography, with additions by Mr. Redpath.

These books are available, and while they are not in all public school libraries, they are in collections at larger central libraries.

Several others gave moral support and encouragement to John Brown. One who was close to him and influenced a large number of people in Brown's behalf was the Reverend Mr. Theodore Parker, Unitarian minister and resident of Boston. It is said that he was one of the first to whom John Brown divulged the details of his Master Plan.

In January of 1858 John Brown visited the ex-slave Frederick Douglass at his home in Rochester and spent several weeks there. Brown attempted to enlist the aid of Douglass. He met another ex-slave in the home of Douglass. This was Shields Green, a fugitive runaway from South Carolina. Green was different from Douglass. He had never learned to read. He seldom spoke and then with only a few blunt words. However, he did have strong feelings, and he bore himself with dignity. Other blacks called him "Emperor." He listened attentively to Brown, and Brown liked him.

They talked with other black men in the area. They

held no large meetings, but there were a number of small conferences and visits. Secrecy surrounded Brown's movements because federal warrants for his arrest had been issued. His activities in Kansas had made him practically an outlaw. John Brown visited Stephen Smith, a rich Negro merchant in Philadelphia. He stayed with Mr. Smith for nearly a week and had additional contact with several black leaders. New York City, New Haven, and Boston were other cities he visited on this trip.

In Boston he took the remarkable ex-slave Harriet Tubman to Wendell Phillips, a well-known abolitionist. Phillips afterward reported that in making the presentation Brown said, "I bring you one of the best and bravest persons on this continent—General Tubman, as we call her."

Harriet Tubman promised to join in the enterprise at Harpers Ferry. At the time of the attack, however, she was very sick and could not join the man she admired so much.

In March of 1858 Brown met in Boston with five of his strongest supporters. The group included Theodore Parker, minister, Franklin Sanborn, teacher, George Stearns, merchant, Samuel Gridley Howe, medical doctor and specialist in treatment of the mentally retarded, and Thomas Wentworth Higginson, another minister. All of these had contributed money as well as time and effort to John Brown. Stearns had shipped guns and other supplies to Kansas.

At this time these five agreed that moral suasion was not going to make slave owners repent and free their slaves. They also recognized that the southern states

Harriet Tubman

would not make laws to do away with the system or even to soften its evils. Although they did not know Brown's point of attack, they believed that direct action was necessary and that John Brown was the man to lead it. These five, together with Gerrit Smith, who was not present at the time, formed themselves into the Committee of the Secret Six.

On March 25 Gerrit Smith wrote, "The slave will be delivered by the shedding of blood, and the signs are multiplying that his deliverance is at hand."

Abraham Lincoln, who was not yet elected to the presidency, would not have been a party to the hopes of the Secret Six. He was saying that slavery was wrong and it should be kept out of the West, but that it was indeed a southern problem and it could be abolished only by southerners themselves. He feared that the spread of slavery with unpaid black workers would lead to lower pay and poverty for white workers. Poor whites in the South were living little better than slaves.

In one of his early speeches Lincoln attacked the absence of logic in the southern position. He said:

> We know Southern men declare that their slaves are better off than hired laborers among us. How little they know whereof they speak! There is no permanent class of hired laborers amongst us. Twenty-five years ago I was a hired laborer. The hired laborer of yesterday labors on his own account today, and will hire others to labor for him tomorrow. Advancement—improvement in condition—is the order of things in a society of equals. . . .
>
> Free labor has the inspiration of hope; pure slavery has no hope. The power of hope upon human exertion and happiness is wonderful.

The Master Plan Develops

In the period between his departure from Kansas and his return in 1858, John Brown was very busy. Several organizations of abolitionists were active. Some gave money directly to Brown. Some shipped food and home-making supplies to free-state settlers, and others sent guns and ammunition to the fighting groups.

In all of this Brown never lost sight of his Master Plan. It had grown and developed through the years. At first he worked with the Underground Railroad. Then he developed the idea of a massive flow of runaways who would be led and supported by a force of fighting men. He believed that a dramatic beginning would arouse the nation and gain continuing support. Nothing could be more dramatic than an attack on Harpers Ferry. No point of beginning could be better located.

Looking upon the Allegheny Mountain range, he said, "God established the Allegheny Mountains from the foundation of the world that they might one day be a refuge for fugitive slaves."

While in Kansas he considered a route northward through the Mississippi Valley as an avenue of escape. He soon gave that up and returned to thinking of the Alleghenies with his North Elba home at one end and with valleys and ridges through Virginia, the Carolinas, and down into Georgia as the lines of escape. Brown did not divulge the whole plan to many people.

One of those to whom he did describe it was John Henry Kagi. The two men first met in Kansas. Kagi was a much younger man than Brown, but a person of unquestionable courage, lofty ideas, and good judgment.

In the Master Plan, Harpers Ferry was established as a point to be seized, but not held. It was to be taken because arms and ammunition were stored there. It was not well guarded. After the capture of Harpers Ferry, the plan was to organize guerrilla bands who would protect slaves as they fled northward. These were to be made up primarily of slave escapees. Some were to be recruited in Canada, others in the northern states. To those recruits would be added, according to the plan, many slaves who would rise up, drop their tools, and rush to the side of the liberation army. It was expected that as the slaves left their masters, the masters themselves would pursue them and that Brown's men, acting in self-defense, would defeat the masters. It was anticipated that the militia would be called out after the masters had been struck down. These, also, Brown felt, could be handled and defeated. He spoke of striking terror into the hearts of the slave states by the strength and skill of his organization. The freed Negroes from the North and those from Canada would inspire confidence in the hearts of those who were still in bondage.

Kagi was told that most of the fighting was to be in the mountains of Virginia, extending down into North Carolina and Tennessee, possibly into the swamps of South Carolina. As a writer and later as a scout for John Brown, Kagi visited many of these areas and knew the land very well.

The blow against Harpers Ferry was to be made in the spring, when the planters were busy and while slaves were badly needed. Telegraph wires would be cut. Railroad tracks would be torn up. Food and supplies would be taken from the farms and establishments of slave owners. Lines of communication toward the North would be protected and kept open.

Those who had been with Brown a long time and who had proven their skill and courage would be commissioned as officers. Both whites and blacks would be officers, as they proved to be skilled and trustworthy. Officers would have the use of pistols and Sharps rifles, the best guns available at that time. The slaves and the fighters would be armed with pikes, muskets, and shotguns. The pike was a spearlike instrument about five feet six inches long and tipped with a sharp metal blade. The pike could be very effective as a weapon.

Kagi stated to friends that he went into this activity believing that sooner or later there would have to be a great uprising among the slaves and a great loss of blood. He believed that if John Brown and his party initiated the uprising, it could be controlled. Without good organization and good control Kagi expected great atrocities. Blacks outnumbered whites in sections of the South. Slaves had attempted uprisings before but they had lacked outside assistance and guidance. At this time there were rumors of a network of slaves prepared to fight for their freedom. John Brown and the leaders in his movement were in touch with some of these groups.

A League of Freedom had been organized in the North. Branches were found all along the borders of Canada, from Syracuse, New York, to Detroit, Michigan. It cooperated with the workers in the Underground Railroad. Only black people were allowed to belong to the League of Freedom.

Brown also counted on the support of the half million black people in the United States who were already free. He knew some of them, such as Harriet Tubman and Frederick Douglass, as close personal friends. The home of Douglass in Rochester, New York, became a resting place for Brown.

Before 1850 a considerable number of black men had been educated in the professions. Some entered business activities and some worked in public employment. One was a librarian at the Cleveland Public Library. Several were schooled at Oberlin College in Ohio.

Even in the South where slavery was legal, a few free Negroes had accumulated wealth, including slaves as well as real estate.

9

Strong Men Organize
in Canada

After his tour of American cities working to secure the support of black people in the United States, Brown moved on to Canada. More than 50,000 free Negroes were living there. They were more or less absorbed in the population. Their children attended school with the Canadian children. The British government had by law made it possible for them to become citizens of the British Empire. Some had taken advantage of this, and they took pride in considering themselves subjects of the king.

Brown hoped to set up strong Canadian backing. He made several visits and held meetings in Toronto and other centers before visiting a well-educated leader in the black population.

Martin R. Delany was a medical doctor and a strong advocate of colonizing Africa. He lived in Chatham, Canada, but he attended several conventions in the United States with Frederick Douglass and others, at all times

urging a plan for moving free blacks beyond the shores
of North America.

"I must see you," John Brown wrote. "I have much
to do and but little time before me."

When he was able to meet with Dr. Delany, he told
him that he had been trying to get the backing of some
large convention or council, and he had been advised
that the doctor would be able to get such support.

"But I am not a man of influence," Delany protested.
"Many of our best people do not believe in my plan. I
tell them that we should return to our motherland, and
they tell me that this is their country now."

"Sir, the people of the northern states are cowards,"
Brown replied. "Slavery has made cowards of them all.
The whites are afraid of each other, and the blacks are
afraid of the whites."

Delany promised to help as much as he could to get
the endorsement of a convention.

"That is all," Brown concluded, "but that is a great
deal to me. It is men I want, and not money. Money I
can get. Money can come without being seen but, men
are afraid of identification with me. . . . They are cowards, sir! Cowards."

Brown described his plan, and Delany promised his
help in organizing a secret convention to be held in
Chatham in 1858.

Delany joined with Brown in issuing the call. Letters
and messengers were dispersed through the part of Canada just north of Lake Erie, where most of the free blacks
resided. It is the southern part of the province of On-
tario. The city of Buffalo in northern New York State
is at the extreme eastern end of the lake and De-

troit, Michigan, at the extreme western end. The city of Chatham is approximately fifty miles east of Detroit.

After meeting people there and establishing plans for the Chatham convention, Brown went back to the States by way of Detroit to bring in some of the leading supporters in his Master Plan. They were fighters who had been with him in Kansas. They had been drilling and maintaining a solid, disciplined organization in Springdale, Iowa, a Quaker settlement.

Those who awaited the call of their leader in Iowa included Owen Brown, a son of John Brown, about thirty-five years of age. He was partially crippled, good-tempered, but cynical.

John Henry Kagi, about twenty-four, was to emerge as Brown's second in command.

John E. Cook, twenty-nine, was an ex-soldier, poet, and reformer.

William H. Leeman, twenty, had been a freedom fighter in Kansas for three years.

Charles Plummer Tidd, twenty-five, of whom it was said that he looked like a fighting man and that his looks were in no way deceptive.

Then there was Aaron Dwight Stevens, about twenty-eight years of age, an ex-soldier. He had left his military unit after having beaten a major. Stevens had been a good fighter with John Brown in Kansas. At Springdale he served as drillmaster through the months that the group was there. He taught military maneuvers and gave to his fellow recruits the benefit of his army training.

Jeremiah Goldsmith Anderson, twenty-six, was swarthy in color. He may have been a mulatto, a mixed blood, but he was considered white.

The two Coppoc brothers, Edwin, twenty-four, and Barclay, nineteen, were not experienced fighters. They were sons of a Quaker widow who lived in Iowa. Barclay was teased by the others because of his youthful appearance. They said he should have spent time with John Brown in Kansas; it would have toughened him up. Both the Coppoc boys later did go with Brown to Harpers Ferry.

Others in the party included Charles Moffett, Luke Parsons, Gill Gaylor, and a black man, Richard Richardson, who had been with Brown in Kansas. These last four, however, did not get to Harpers Ferry.

With this band, most of whom were experienced fighters, John Brown returned to Chatham, where he was received with great interest by those gathered for the convention.

One of those in Chatham was Osborn Perry Anderson, at this time about twenty-four years old. Anderson, who had been born free in Pennsylvania, had migrated to Canada. He was educated and he was skilled as a printer. John Brown used him as a leading person in the group, and Anderson served as secretary in many situations.

Later Anderson wrote about his impressions of John Brown:

> Where ever he went around, although an entire stranger he made a profound impression upon those who saw or became acquainted with him. Some supposed him a staid but modernized Quaker, others a solid business man from "somewhere," and without question a philanthropist. His long white beard, thoughtful and reverent brow and physiognomy, his sturdy, measured tread, as he circulated with hands un-

der the pendant coat skirts of plain brown tweed, with other garments to match, revived to those honored with his acquaintance and knowing his history, the memory of a puritan of the most exalted type.

One man whom John Brown had not seen before drew Brown aside and said that a Mrs. Ellen Smith wanted to talk with him privately. She was waiting at a local hotel. Brown could not immediately break away from others, but at the end of the day he went with the messenger, who said very little about the lady.

On entering the room they faced a well-dressed woman who seemed to be perfectly at ease as she invited him to be seated. Then she explained that she had heard so much about Captain Brown's work that she and some of her friends wanted to know how they might help. She lost her composure, however, when Brown told her that he had seen her once before. She had joined him in hiding and protecting a runaway slave.

"It was in Ohio," he said, "on a farm near Akron."

"Yes, yes," she answered. "Now I remember. You were the neighbor who brought the black man to Mr. Howard's house asking for shelter. You said the slave catchers were closing in on you and the runaway."

"That's right. And you and Mrs. Howard hid the man under the table. When the slave catchers came to the door you ladies were sitting there eating your breakfast and your skirts were spread out wide."

There were other details they recalled. Then John Brown said, "I knew how you felt about helping runaways, so I know now that we can trust you."

"Yes, but there was something you did not know."

She rose from her seat and went across the room to sit beside the man who had brought Brown to the hotel.

"I am not a white woman," she said, "and when you saw me in Ohio I was a runaway myself. Because of my light color and advantages of schooling it was not difficult for me to pass for white."

She told Brown that her name was Mary Ellen Pleasant and the man beside her was her husband, John Pleasant. He too was very light. They lived in San Francisco, where they had prospered in employment and in business.

"Now we want to help," she said as she took a leather pouch out of a traveling bag and handed it to Brown. "Friends in San Francisco, ex-slaves and some free-born blacks sent this poke of gold to you. They asked that I tell you they will send more."

"We have brought money for you too," John Pleasant said. "And we will give more. Now we want to help with ourselves. We can both pass for white. There must be things we can do."

The three of them sat talking far into the night.

Brown said that he hoped to provide weapons and leadership for slaves, helping them to escape from their masters and to move northward in large numbers.

John Pleasant expressed doubts.

"I don't believe the slaves are ready to act on such a plan," he said. "They've been under the lash all their lives. Most of them don't dare think about resistance."

Brown was quick to say that his people had been working on that problem, and he spoke of uprisings that had already taken place in many southern states. He stressed that he could provide plenty of trained leadership and plenty of arms with which the runaways could defend themselves.

Then Brown told them about the rifle works and the arsenal at Harpers Ferry.

"But that's United States government," Mary Pleasant said. "It's the army and all the power of the nation. I don't see how you could hope to succeed."

Brown insisted that his plans were well thought out and that with God's help they would destroy the monster of slavery.

Mary Ellen Pleasant and her husband were well known in San Francisco, where they had acquired valuable real estate and other assets. They had brought with them $1,500 in addition to $500 in gold contributed by friends. Also, Mary Pleasant had arranged for a bank draft of $30,000 to be forwarded to her. She did not tell Brown about the money waiting for her order. She wanted first to be sure about Brown's plan. The idea of attacking the installations at Harpers Ferry did not seem practical. However, with Brown's hearty approval, she left Chatham the next day to go to the Harpers Ferry area hoping to spread word among the slaves that good men were organizing to help them gain their freedom.

The first formal meeting of the entire convention was in the Baptist church. The pastor of the church, the Reverend William Charles Munroe, was elected president. John Henry Kagi and Osborn Anderson acted as secretaries. John Brown was presented to make an opening statement. Brown spoke briefly, and then he presented the new national constitution. This was to some extent based on a covenant which had been signed during the guerrilla warfare in Kansas. Many of the provisions were accepted without any discussion or debate. However, the following article faced objection: "The foregoing articles shall not be so as in any way to encourage the overthrow of any state government or general government of the United States, and look to no dissolution of the Union, but simply to amendment and appeal, and all flags shall be the same as our fathers fought for under the revolution."

One of the ex-slaves who had achieved his freedom in Canada said that he felt no allegiance to the nation that had robbed and humiliated him. However, others wanted the article, and it passed. Finally the constitution itself was adopted.

The constitution, consisting of forty-eight articles, provided for a national congress, a president, and a court. All the officials were to unite and select a commander-in-chief, a treasurer, a secretary, and other officials. No salaries were to be paid. All officers were to support themselves at other jobs or in farming or business. Schools and churches were to be established.

John Brown wrote home: "Had a good abolition convention here, from different parts. . . . Constitution slightly amended and adopted, and society organized."

The convention also discussed some other matters.

An ex-slave, James M. Jones, brought up the matter of slaves in the southland joining in the freedom movement as John Brown had described his plan. Jones said that Brown would be disappointed. He pointed out that the slaves did not know enough about the plan to rally to his support. This may have been prophetic. The events at Harpers Ferry in the following year would indicate that Jones understood that the American slave system robbed its victims of hope and of will power. But John Brown would not accept the possibility of failure.

There were other discussions with regard to the time of striking the blow. This convention was held in May, and Brown was eager to get on with his plan, even hoping it could be accomplished during the summer of the same year, 1858. Some, calling for delay, suggested that no action be taken until the United States should be engaged in war with another foreign power. Brown vigorously opposed such a thought.

"I would be the last one to take advantage of my country in the face of a foreign foe," he said.

During all of the convention Brown did not lay out the details of his plan. He had to organize additional support. He also had to overcome the work of a traitor within the small group he had organized.

Brown had made an alliance with Hugh Forbes. This man was an adventurer, a soldier of fortune. English by birth, Forbes had lived in Italy and fought there. He claimed to be skilled in the art of war, and some of Brown's friends recommended him as a man who would be very valuable in the planned action. Forbes succeeded in selling himself to Brown, who paid him for services and gave him money for printing a manual to be used in training the fighters with the John Brown force.

For several weeks before the convention in Chatham, Forbes had been voicing complaints among Brown's supporters. Forbes was angry. He said he was without

Hugh Forbes

funds. He claimed he had been dealt with badly. He demanded that he be placed in charge of the abolition action. He threatened to go to the United States government and disclose the plans. In fact, it is clear that he did make the plan known to certain government officials. Fortunately for Brown, these people did not act upon the information. Some of Brown's supporters were shaken. They spoke of abandoning the whole program.

Forbes wrote, "I have been grossly defrauded in the name of humanity and anti-slavery. I have for years labored in the anti-slavery cause without wanting or thinking of recompense. Though I have made the least possible parade of my work, it has nevertheless not been entirely without fruit . . . patience and mild measures have failed. I reluctantly have recourse to harshness."

John Brown had news of this before he left the convention in May 1858. He went ahead with his plans, however, and tried to deal gently with Forbes. Some of the supplies which had been sent to Brown for the fighting in Kansas were in storage. Forbes knew the hiding places. These had to be removed at once.

There can be no doubt that the affair of Hugh Forbes delayed the movement toward Harpers Ferry by at least one year.

After the convention the fighters scattered. Some of them found jobs in northern Ohio. Kagi, who was an expert printer, went to Hamilton, Canada, where he set up type and printed copies of the constitution. John Cook went immediately to Harpers Ferry, where he got a job as a lock tender in the canal system. In the meantime, Brown went back to New York and to Boston to try to rally the support of his backers and to overcome the destructive work of Forbes. Later, Brown and several others of his group returned to Kansas, where they tried to recruit new help and where they secured their stock of guns and ammunition. They moved the supplies eastward and stored them in new hiding places.

10

Brown Returns to Kansas

Indeed, Brown's work in Kansas was not yet completed. In May 1858 a slave-stater from Georgia organized a large band of men. They rounded up eleven free-staters and proceeded to massacre them in what was known as the Marais des Cygnes Massacre. They thought they had killed them all, but five recovered from their wounds and escaped.

When the news of this incident reached Brown in the East, he went back to Kansas and moved into the area of the massacre. Some of his former companions rallied to his support. They reorganized under the name Shubel Morgan's Company. The company was also known as Morgan's Raiders. Brown called himself Shubel Morgan.

Brown and this company fought on the side of Captain James Montgomery, a leader in the remaining vestiges of the local warfare. With the coming of winter, the cold weather made fighting impractical, but it brought

The Marais des Cygnes Massacre, Kansas, May 19, 1858.

to Brown a second major opportunity to strike a blow
for freedom.

Later he wrote about that event. His report was published in the *New York Tribune.*

> On Sunday, December 19th, a Negro man called Jim
> came over to Osage settlement, from Missouri, and
> stated that he, together with his wife, two children,
> and another Negro man, was to be sold within a day
> or two, and begged for help to get away. On Monday
> (the following) night, two small companies were made
> up to go to Missouri and forcibly liberate the five slaves,
> together with other slaves. One of these companies I
> assumed to direct. We proceeded to the place, sur-
> rounded the building, liberated the slaves, and also
> took certain property supposed to belong to the estate.
> We, however, learned before leaving that a portion
> of the articles we had, belonged to a man living on
> the plantation as a tenant, and who was supposed to

have no interest in the estate. We promptly returned
to him all we had taken. We then went to another plantation, where we found five more slaves, took some
property and two white men. We all moved slowly away
into the Territory for some distance, and then sent
the white men back, telling them to follow us as soon
as they chose to do so. The other company freed one
female slave, took some property, and, as I am in-
formed, killed one white man (the master), who fought
against the liberation.

Now for comparison. Eleven persons are forcibly restored to their natural and inalienable rights, with but
one man killed, and all "hell is stirred from beneath."
It is currently reported that the governor of Missouri
has made a requisition upon the governor of Kansas
for the delivery of all such as were concerned in the
last named "dreadful outrage." The marshall of Kansas
is said to be collecting a posse of Missouri (not Kansas)
men at West Point, in Missouri, a little town about
ten miles distant to "enforce the laws."

One of the slaves, Samuel Harper, afterward told this
story of the thousand-mile trip from Kansas to Canada.

It was mighty slow traveling. You see there were several
different parties amongst our band, and our masters
had people looking all over for us. We would ride all
night, and then maybe, we would have to stay several
days in one house to keep from getting caught. In a
month we had only got to a place near Topeka, which
was about forty miles from where we started. There
was twelve of us at the one house of a man named
Doyle, besides the captain and his men, when there

came along a gang of slave-hunters. One of Captain Brown's men, Stevens, he went down to them and said: "Gentlemen, you look as if you were looking for somebody or something." "Aye, yes!" says the leader, "we think as how you have some of our slaves up yonder in that there house." "Is that so?" says Stevens. "Well, come right along with me, and you can look them over and see."

We were watching this here conversation all the time, and when we see Stevens coming up to the house with that there man, we just didn't know what to make of it. We began to get scared that Stevens was going to give us to them slave-hunters. But the look of things changed when Stevens got up to the house. He just opened the door long enough for to grab a double-barreled gun. He pointed it at the slave-hunter, and says: "You want to see your slaves, does you? Well, just look up them barrels and see if you can find them." The man just went all to pieces. He dropped his gun, his legs went trembling, and the tears most started from his eyes. Stevens took and locked him up in the house. When the rest of the crowd see him captured, they ran away as fast as they could go.

Captain Brown went to see the prisoner, and says to him, "I'll show you what it is to look after slaves, my man." That frightened the prisoner awful. He was a kind of a old fellow and when he heard what the captain said, I suppose he thought he was going to be killed. He began to cry and beg to be let go. The captain he only smiled a little bit, and talked some more to him, and the next day he was let go.

A few days afterwards, the United States marshall came up with another gang to capture us. There was about seventy-five of them, and they surrounded the house, and we was all afraid we was going to be took for sure. But the captain he just said, "Get ready, boys, and we'll ship them all." There was only fourteen of us altogether, but the captain was a terror to them, and when he stepped out of the house and went for them the whole seventy-five of them started running. Captain Brown and Kagi and some of the others chased them, and captured five prisoners. There was a doctor and lawyer amongst them. They all had nice horses. The captain made them get down. Then he told five of us slaves to mount the beasts and we rode them while the white men had to walk. It was early spring, and the mud on the roads was away over their ankles. I just tell you it was mighty tough walking, and you can believe those fellows had enough slave-hunting. The next day the captain let them go.

Our masters kept spies watching till we crossed the border. When we got to Springdale, Ia., a man came to see Captain Brown, and told him there was a lot of friends down in a town in Kansas that wanted to see him. The captain said he did not care to go down, but as soon as the man started back Captain Brown followed him. When he came back, he said there was a crowd coming up to capture us. We all went up to the schoolhouse and got ourselves ready to fight.

The crowd came and hung around the schoolhouse a few days, but they didn't try to capture us. The governor of Kansas, he telegraphed to the United States marshall at Springdale: "Capture John Brown, dead or alive." The marshall, he answered: "If I try to capture John Brown it'll be dead, and I'll be the one that'll be dead." Finally those Kansas people went home, and then that same marshall put us in a car* and sent us

* A railway car, probably a boxcar.

to Chicago. It took us over three months to get to
Canada. . . .

What kind of a man was Captain Brown? He was a
great big man, over six feet tall, with great big shoul-
ders, and long hair, white as snow. He was a very quiet
man, awful quiet. He never even laughed. After we
was free we was wild of course, and we used to cut
up all kinds of foolishness. But the captain would always
look solemn as a graveyard. Sometime he just let out
the tiniest bit of a smile and says: "You'd better quit
your fooling and take up your book."

11

On to Harpers Ferry

In 1859 the town of Harpers Ferry in Jefferson County, Virginia, had a population of about 2500 people. It was about fifty-seven miles northwest of the nation's capital, Washington, D.C. Chambersburg was about fifty miles to the north in Pennsylvania, which was a free state. About a hundred years earlier, an English immigrant named Robert Harper, who was an architect and builder, operated a ferry across the Potomac River here. This is the place where the Shenandoah River, flowing eastward, spills into the Potomac River, which is flowing southward. The town of Harpers Ferry is at the bottom of the V-shaped peninsula between the rivers. The two rivers cut through the Blue Ridge Mountains, a section of the Appalachians.

During John Brown's time the Potomac River formed the dividing line between Maryland, on the east, and Virginia, on the west. Later, during the Civil War, the western area of Virginia did not go along with the major part of the state in withdrawing from the United States. That was the beginning of the state of West Virginia. Today the extreme eastern point of West Virginia is the peninsula with the town of Harpers Ferry.

Across the two rivers, bluffs rise to the height of nearly a thousand feet. These slopes are very rocky. They are covered with small brush and some large trees.

The Baltimore and Ohio Railroad bridge crosses the Potomac between Harpers Ferry and the Maryland side.

A view of Harpers Ferry showing the covered railroad bridge and, in the distance, the United States arsenal.

A hundred years ago the bridge was covered. It carried not only the railway tracks but also the wagon road. In those days, also, barges were used on the river. To protect them from rocks, channels had been dug parallel to the river to form canals. Horses and mules pulled the barges along these canals. Remnants of these canals are still visible.

Along the Potomac side of the town of Harpers Ferry were twenty brick-and-stone buildings. They were factories and shops making large guns, military vehicles, and specialized equipment. A high wall with iron gates protected the area, which was known as the armory.

Guns and equipment were stored in other buildings in an enclosure that was called the arsenal. The arsenal was nearer the point where the Shenandoah River flows into the Potomac.

A plank bridge carried a roadway from the town across the Shenandoah. Other bridges connected the town to islands in the river, the largest of which was Virginius Island. The swiftly moving waters of the river provided tremendous water power. A four-story cotton mill was one of the factories on the island that used this power. Another factory on the island was very important to Brown. It was the federal rifle works.

This area was originally selected by George Washington and Thomas Jefferson as a place for manufacture and storage of guns and military equipment. Most of the men of Harpers Ferry were employed in the mills and factories and warehouses.

It is surprising that no soldiers were on duty. The employees were civilians. The watchmen were not well armed and they were untrained. John Brown was aware

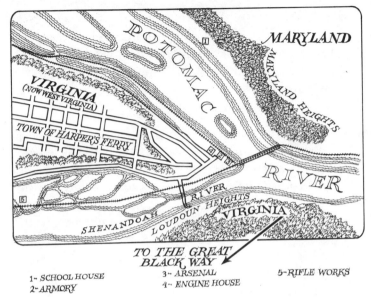

1- SCHOOL HOUSE 2- ARMORY 3- ARSENAL 4- ENGINE HOUSE 5- RIFLE WORKS

A map of the town of Harpers Ferry and the land around it where the Potomac and Shenandoah rivers come together. The numbers indicate places that figured in John Brown's raid. The arrow points south toward the Great Black Way— the Appalachian Mountains Brown planned to use as his stronghold.

of these details. The armory on the bank of the Potomac, the arsenal at the point, and the rifle factory on Virginius Island in the Shenandoah—each of these units was part of John Brown's Master Plan.

More than a year passed after the convention at Chatham before Brown moved toward Harpers Ferry. He had been sick, and he had been busy with trips to Kansas and back to the East again. He had consulted his friends in New York and New England, where he bought supplies as fast and sometimes faster than he collected money.

Some writers say that fantastic amounts were given to Brown. It is true that many people believed in him, but his efforts were limited. He was a wanted man. He could not appear in public meetings, and he could not openly announce plans.

Richard J. Hinton wrote that

> as near as can be estimated, the money received by Brown could not have exceeded $12,000 while the supplies, arms, etc., furnished may have cost $10,000 more. Of course, there were smaller contributions and support coming in, but if the total estimate be placed at $25,000 for the period between the 15th of September 1856 when he left Lawrence, Kansas, and the 16th of October 1859 when he moved on Harpers Ferry, Virginia, with twenty-one men, it would certainly cover all the outlay except that of time, labor, and lives.

In the month of May 1858, immediately after the convention in Chatham, one of Brown's most reliable men, John Cook, had gone southward to the area of Harpers Ferry. There he established himself as a dealer in books and maps. He also took a job as a watchman on the canal locks near Harpers Ferry. By nature, Cook was a very likable person and something of a poet. It is not surprising that he fell in love with and married a local girl.

His job, his wife, and his part-time activities as a salesman made him a most valuable front-runner for the expedition.

Over a year later, on June 20, 1859, the advance guard of five—John Brown with two sons, Oliver and Owen, Jeremiah Anderson and John Henri Kagi—started southward.

The party arrived at Chambersburg, Pennsylvania, where a free black named Watson, a barber, helped them get established. Watson was active with the Underground Railroad. He was well acquainted with the area and he knew whites who could be trusted as friends. John Henri Kagi was set up as a general agent to work with men and materials as they came southward.

On July 3, 1859, the party without Kagi arrived at Harpers Ferry. They saw Cook, but they did not speak to him openly or show that they knew him.

John Brown, now using the name of Isaac Smith, went about with his sons and Anderson. They gave the appearance of newcomers looking for a place to settle. A local farmer met them and, after an initial greeting, said, "I suppose you're out hunting minerals, gold, and silver?"

Brown answered, "No, we are not. We're out looking for land. We want to buy land. We have a little money, but we want to make it go as far as we can."

He asked the price of land in the area, and the local farmer told him that it ranged from fifteen to thirty dollars an acre.

Brown remarked, "That is high. I thought I could buy land here for about one or two dollars per acre."

The farmer answered, "No, sir. If you expect to get land for that price you will have to go further west, to Kansas or some of those territories where there is government land."

The farmer then asked him where he came from. Brown answered, "From the northern part of the state of New York."

The farmer asked what his activity was there, his occupation. Brown answered that he was a farmer but that the frost had been so heavy lately that it had reduced his crops. He felt that he wanted to make a new start. He had sold out and moved farther south. He said he was undecided as to whether he should buy land or cattle. He thought he might rent some land and purchase cattle which he might develop into valuable stock.

From this farmer and from others, Brown (alias Smith) gained valuable information. Finally he rented a piece of property from a family named Kennedy. He paid thirty-five dollars rent for the coming season of nine months.

This farm, referred to in most of the accounts as the Kennedy farm, was between four and five miles north of Harpers Ferry in Maryland on the road to Chambersburg. The house was about three hundred yards back from the highway. It was in plain sight. However, farther away on the other side of a hill was another cabin with one room and a garret. This was not visible from the highway. Brown settled there with his party. The farm became the assembly place not only for his men but for his materials, including the guns, which were slow in coming, and a thousand pikes from Connecticut. Brown asked Anne, his daughter, and Martha, the wife of Oliver, to come and keep house. They were on the farm doing the cooking and most of the household work from the middle of July until the last of September.

According to later reports from those in the community and from the writings of those who were present, there was a high level of activity at the farm for several months.

**The Kennedy farm in Washington County, Maryland,
where John Brown and his band prepared for their raid on Harpers Ferry.**

In the north, John Jr. was collecting and shipping arms and gathering men and money.

Kagi was making headquarters at Chambersburg.

Brown himself labored and traveled day and night, sometimes riding on old Dolly, his mule, and sometimes in the wagon. He made many fifty-mile trips between the farm and Chambersburg.

By August there were at Harpers Ferry the two young women; three of Brown's sons—Oliver, Owen, and Watson; the two young Coppoc brothers, Barclay and Edwin, sons of the Quaker widow in Iowa; the Thompson brothers, Dauphin and William; Charles Tidd; Jerry Anderson; Aaron Stevens; Albert Hazlett; William Leeman;

Stewart Taylor; and Dangerfield Newby, a black man.

Newby, whose wife, Harriet, was a slave living thirty miles south of Harpers Ferry, was risking his life to be on Virginia soil. It was a crime, punishable by death, and certainly punishable by return to slavery, for a free black to enter the state of Virginia.

Hazlett, Indiana born, was at this time about twenty-three years of age. He had gone to Kansas and participated in the fighting there. He had joined Brown's company in 1858, and he had helped to escort the rescued slaves to Canada. After that he stayed a short time in northern Ohio and then returned to Pennsylvania, where he remained at his brother's place until the summer of 1859 when he went to the Kennedy farm.

In May, while Hazlett was waiting with his brother in Ohio, he wrote to John Brown: "I wish it would come up soon. I'm tired of doing nothing."

Again in July he wrote: "I will be ready when you want me."

He was said to be a bright, kindly, obliging young man, always frank and willing. In appearance, he was about five feet eleven inches in height, slender, with a well-shaped head, oval face, very fair complexion, blond, curly hair; he had an open expression; was genial, and brave to the last degree.

John Brown tried to get Frederick Douglass to be with him at Harpers Ferry. He had disclosed a part of the Master Plan to Douglass, and he had said to him that it would be by force, and only by the shedding of blood, that slavery would be abolished.

We know a great deal about this relationship because it has been described by Frederick Douglass. It has been repeated in many of the writings that are included in the bibliography of this book. A three-act stage play, *In Splendid Error,* by William Branch dramatizes this relationship. It expresses the feeling of Frederick Douglass that Brown was indeed mistaken in his effort although his mistake was one of splendid error.

Brown sent word to Douglass at his home and asked him to come. He wanted to talk with him one more time. After an exchange of letters a meeting was arranged.

Douglass appeared at Chambersburg. He brought with him the escaped slave, Shields Green. They met in an abandoned stone quarry on the edge of the town.

Douglass later wrote that Brown had pretended to be fishing. His hat was old and storm-beaten, and his clothes were the color of the quarry itself. Here is the story as written by Frederick Douglass:

> His face wore an anxious expression, and he was much worn by thought and exposure. I felt that I was on a dangerous mission, and was as little desirous of discovery as himself, 'though no reward had been offered for me. We, Mr. Kagi, Captain Brown, Shields Green, and myself sat down among the rocks and talked over the enterprise which was about to be undertaken. The taking of Harpers Ferry, of which Captain Brown had merely hinted before, was now declared as his settled purpose, and he wanted to know what I thought of it. I at once opposed the measure with all the arguments at my command. To me, such a measure would be fatal to running off slaves (as was the original plan), and fatal to all engaged in doing so. It would be an attack upon the Federal government, and would array

the whole country against us. Captain Brown did most
of the talking on the other side of the question. He
did not at all object to rousing the nation; it seemed
to him that something startling was just what the nation
needed. . . . Our talk was long and earnest; we spent
most of Saturday and a part of Sunday in this debate—
Brown for Harpers Ferry, and I against it; he for striking
a blow which should instantly rouse the country, and
I for the policy of gradually and unaccountably drawing
off the slaves to the mountains, as at first suggested
and proposed by him. When I found that he had fully
made up his mind and could not be dissuaded, I turned
to Shields Green and told him he heard what Captain
Brown had said; his old plan was changed, and that I
should return home, and if he wished to go with me
he could do so. Captain Brown urged us both to go
with him but I could not do so, and could but feel
that he was about to rivet the fetters more firmly than
ever on the limbs of the enslaved. In parting he put
his arms around me in a manner more than friendly,
and said: "Come with me, Douglass, I will defend you
with my life. I want you for a special purpose. When
I strike, the bees* will begin to swarm, and I shall want
you to help hive them!"

But my discretion or my cowardice made me proof
against the dear old man's eloquence—perhaps it was
something of both which determined my course. When
about to leave, I asked Green what he had decided
to do, and was surprised by his coolly saying, in his
broken way, "I b'lieve I'll go wid de old man."

* Brown here referred to liberated slaves, believing that immediately after his action they would be swarming like bees; they would
need leadership; Brown believed that Douglass could lead and organize them.

Here we separated; they to go to Harpers Ferry, I to Rochester.

Who can say whether it was discretion or cowardice that made Douglass reject Brown's plea for help.

And what if Frederick Douglass had gone with John Brown to Harpers Ferry? Would he have changed the course of events?

The Kennedy farm was well located for Brown's purposes, but for those who assembled there life was tense. The danger of discovery was very real. Discipline was necessarily harsh. The waiting was monotonous.

Two who were there have left descriptions of life there.

Anne Brown, John Brown's daughter, included the following in her account of her last days with her father.

> There was a family of poor people who lived near by and who had rented the garden on the Kennedy place, directly back of the house. The little barefooted woman and four small children (she carried the youngest in her arms) would all come trooping over to the garden at all hours of the day, and, at times, several times during the day. Nearly always they would come up the steps and into the house and stay a short time. This made it very troublesome for us, compelling the men, when she came in sight at mealtimes, to gather up the victuals and table cloth and quietly disappear upstairs.
>
> One Saturday, father and I went to a religious meeting that was held in a grove near the schoolhouse, and the folks left at home forgot to keep a sharp lookout for Mrs. Heiffmaster, and she stole into the house before they saw her, and saw Shields Green (that must

have been in September), Barclay Coppoc, and Will Leeman. And another time after that she saw C. P. Tidd standing on the porch. She thought these strangers were running off Negroes to the north. I used to give her everything she wanted or asked for to keep her on good terms, but we were in constant fear that she was either a spy or would betray us. It was like standing on a powder magazine, after a slow match had been lighted.

Osborn Anderson also wrote about life at the Kennedy farm.

There was no milk and water sentimentality—no offensive contempt for the Negro, while working in his cause; the pulsations of each and every heart beat in harmony for the suffering and pleading slave . . . In John Brown's house, and in John Brown's presence, men from widely different parts of the continent met and united into one company, wherein no hateful prejudice dared intrude its ugly self—no ghost of distinction found space to enter. . . .

Rough, unsightly, and aged, it was only for those privileged to enter (the house) and tarry for a long time, and to penetrate the mysteries of the two rooms it contained—kitchen, parlor, dining room below, and the spacious chamber, attic, storeroom, prison, drilling-room, comprised in the loft above—who could tell how we lived at Kennedy Farm.

Every morning, when the noble old man was at home, he called the family around, read from his Bible, and offered to God most fervent and touching supplications for all flesh; and especially pathetic were his petitions in behalf of the oppressed. I never heard John Brown pray, that he did not make strong appeals to God for the deliverance of the slave. This duty over, the men went to the loft, there to remain all day long. . . .

Besides the daughter and the daughter-in-law, who superintended the work, some one or other of the men was regularly detailed to assist in the cooking, washing, and other domestic work. After the ladies left we did all the work, no one being exempt, because of age or official grade in the organization.

The principal employment of the prisoners, as we severally were when compelled to stay in the loft, was to study Forbes's Manual, and to go through a quiet, though rapid drill, under the training of Captain Stevens, at some times. At other times we applied a preparation for bronzing our gun barrels—discussed subjects of reform, related our personal history; but when our resources became pretty well exhausted, the *ennui* from confinement, imposed silence, etc., would make the men almost desperate. At such times, neither slavery nor slaveholders were discussed mincingly. We were, while the ladies remained, often relieved of much of the dullness growing out of restraint by their kindness. As we could not circulate freely, they would bring in wild fruit and flowers from the woods and fields.

Two free black men, Lewis Sheridan Leary and John Anthony Copeland, arrived from Oberlin, and a white man, Francis Jackson Meriam, came from Boston.

Lewis Leary, about twenty-four years old, was born a slave in North Carolina. His father was an Irishman named O'Leary. While Lewis was very young, his father moved to Ohio and took his children with him where they grew up as free people. Lewis Leary was a harness maker. Active in the abolition movement, he wanted to strike a blow to destroy the slave system. He left behind him a wife and a six-month-old baby daughter. He was never to see them again.

John Anthony Copeland, 25, was a student at Oberlin College. He was very light in color. Born free in a community of light-colored people in North Carolina, he was yet willing to give up his security to go back into the South to fight.

Francis Jackson Meriam, twenty-two, was a grandson of the president of the American Anti-Slavery Society. He was asked to give some money to help John Brown; then he decided to give his money and himself. He arrived with $600 in cash, and he made a will in which he left all his assets to the Anti-Slavery Society.

The company consisted of twenty-two men in all, seventeen white and five black. John Brown, known as Isaac Smith, by this time was well acquainted with the area and with the people there. All of them, except John Cook, were at the Kennedy farm. Cook was living in the town with his wife and baby.

Some of the local people were suspicious of what might be happening at the farm, but they saw no reason to be alarmed. The slaves saw the man they knew as Captain Isaac Smith going in and out of the homes of slave owners. To the blacks he was just another white man. They had no way of knowing that he was a lover of freedom and that he had a Master Plan to achieve their freedom.

By Saturday, October 15, the day before the actual attack, the situation was tense. Warnings had been given to the federal government, but they were ignored. John Brown, aware that someone in the government might accept the warnings and make investigations, was alert. It was uncommonly calm. John Brown was ready.

John Brown's 21 Men at Harper's Ferry

October 16, 1859

Anderson, Jeremiah
Goldsmith, 26,
born in Indiana,
served with Brown in
Kansas, killed in the raid.

Anderson, Osborn Perry, 29,
born free in
Pennsylvania,
educated at Oberlin,
printer by trade, met
Brown in Canada,
escaped during the
raid, wrote an
eyewitness account,
served in the Civil
War, died in 1871.

Brown, Oliver, 20,
son of John Brown,
served in Kansas,
killed in the raid.

Brown, Owen, 35,
son of John Brown,
served in Kansas,
escaped during the raid.

Brown, Watson, 24
son of John Brown,
stayed on the farm at
North Elba while his
father and others were
in Kansas, killed in the raid.

Cook, John E., 29,
poet and former law
student, met Brown in
Kansas, escaped
during the raid but
was captured and
hanged.

Copeland, John A., Jr., 25,
born free in North
Carolina, lived in
Ohio and attended
Oberlin, carpenter by
trade, captured during
the raid and hanged.

Coppoc, Barclay, 19,
son of a Quaker widow
in Iowa, escaped
during the raid and
later fought in the
Civil War.

Coppoc, Edwin, 24,
brother of Barclay
Coppoc, captured and
hanged.

Green, Shields (nickname Emperor), about 23, ran away from slave life in South Carolina, met John Brown in home of Frederick Douglass, captured and hanged.

Hazlett, Albert, 23, fought in Kansas, escaped during the raid but was captured and hanged.

Kagi, John Henry, 24, former teacher in Virginia, met Brown in Kansas and later became Brown's first assistant, killed during the raid.

Leary, Lewis Sheridan, 24, born a slave in North Carolina, freed by his father who was white, harness maker by trade, killed with John Henry Kagi in the raid. His widow later became the grandmother of the poet Langston Hughes.

Leeman, William H., 20, joined Brown in Kansas, killed with Kagi in the raid.

Meriam, Francis Jackson, 22, New England aristocrat and abolitionist, first met Brown in Virginia, escaped during the raid, served as captain of a black infantry company during the Civil War.

Newby, Dangerfield, 44,
born a slave in
Virginia and later
freed by his white
father, joined Brown
in Virginia, killed in
the raid.

Stevens, Aaron Dwight, 28,
exsoldier, met Brown
in Kansas, taught
military tactics to the
others, wounded and
captured during the
raid, later hanged.

Taylor, Stewart, 23,
Canadian wagon
maker, killed during
the raid.

Thompson, Dauphin
Osgood, 21,
brother of Henry
Thompson, (who was
married to Brown's
daughter Ruth), killed
during the raid.

Thompson, William, 26,
older brother of
Dauphin, killed
during the raid.

Tidd, Charles Plummer, 25,
fought in Kansas,
escaped during raid
and later fought in the
Civil War.

12

Attack!

John Brown did not discuss his plans in detail with anyone. He did not take friends into full confidence. He had told some of his people that the blow would be struck on October 24. It took place on October 16.

One of his most trusted friends, Richard J. Hinton, whom he had known in Kansas as well as in the East, was on the way to join the party at Harpers Ferry. He did not arrive in time. It is also known that some of the free blacks from Canada and from Ohio and New York would have been with him a week later.

Sunday, October 16, 1859.

Brown arose earlier than usual. He assembled his men for prayer as was his practice on every Sabbath morning.

He read a chapter from the Bible.

He offered a fervent prayer asking God "to assist in the liberation of the bondsmen in that slaveholding land." The services were impressive.

All there felt that the time for action had come. In

the early afternoon, Brown called a council meeting. Osborn Anderson presided. Anderson again read the constitution, and those who had not sworn allegiance to it were then offered the opportunity to make their oaths.

In the late afternoon the group was gathered again, and the final orders were given. Stations were designated.

Owen Brown, Francis Meriam, and Barclay Coppoc were to remain at the farm. They were later to deliver the guns, ammunition, and pikes to a schoolhouse across the river from Harpers Ferry.

Charles Tidd and John Cook were to cut the telegraph lines from Harpers Ferry leading toward Washington, D.C.

John Kagi and Aaron Stevens were to capture and hold the guard at the bridge going across the Potomac to Harpers Ferry. Watson Brown and Stewart Taylor were to assist in holding that bridge.

Oliver Brown and William Thompson were to take the other bridge, the one leading from Harpers Ferry across the Shenandoah River.

Jerry Anderson and Dauphin Thompson were to occupy the engine house in the walled enclosure of the armory.

Albert Hazlett and Edwin Coppoc were to hold the arsenal.

After taking the town and the armory with the engine house and the arsenal, Kagi and Copeland were to lead a party to the rifle factory on the island in the Shenandoah River. They were to seize the factory and guard it.

Others were given tasks regarding rounding up prisoners in the town.

Just before moving out, while rain fell softly on the roof and dripped steadily from the eaves, John Brown, in the light of lanterns, addressed his men.

"And now, gentlemen," he said, "let me impress this one thing upon your minds. You all know how dear life is to you, and you know how dear your life is to your friends. And in remembering that, consider the lives of others are as dear to them as yours are to you. Do not, therefore, take the life of anyone if you can possibly avoid it. But if it is necessary to take life in order to save your own, then make sure work of it."

They left the Kennedy farm at eight o'clock that night. The horse-drawn wagon was loaded with guns and pikes, a sledgehammer, and a crowbar. Two men were far ahead of the party, two men were at the head of the horses, and two men brought up the rear. Others came on, two-by-two, at intervals. They moved in somber quiet. They met no other travelers. It took approximately two hours to travel the five miles over the rolling hills, through the woods, across the fords and down to the Potomac.

At about ten Kagi and Stevens took the lead. They reached the covered bridge that crossed the Potomac River from Maryland to Virginia. They took the bridge guard by surprise and made him their prisoner. As the party moved across the river, Tidd and Cook cut the telegraph wires that connected Harpers Ferry to Washington, D.C.

On the Virginia side the party moved up the hill to the armory. At the gate they seized the unarmed watchman and demanded that he open it. He refused. One of the men jumped on the tier of the gate and others clambered across the wall. Not finding the key to the lock, they broke open the gate with a crowbar and a large hammer from the wagon.

"This is a slave state," Brown said to the watchman. "I want to free all the Negroes. . . . If the citizens interfere with me I must only burn the town and have blood."

People of the town passing by saw what was happening, but they did not understand. Frightened, they ran to the Wager House, a nearby hotel, and spread the alarm.

Kagi and Copeland moved swiftly. On the south side of town on the island in the Shenandoah River, they captured the watchman of the rifle works and took possession. Stevens and selected men set out as planned to capture prisoners among the citizens. There was no shooting at all. As they met slaves along the road, they told them what was happening. Stevens asked them to go to the other slaves and to circulate the news. Soon many blacks gathered at the arsenal and the armory.

Among those whom Brown wanted to capture was Colonel Lewis W. Washington, a relative of George Washington. Colonel Washington had once shown Cook his swords and guns. He lived on a farm at some distance from the town. Stevens led a party there, taking with him Leary, Green, and Anderson.

"You are free," Anderson told the slaves at Colonel Washington's farm.

An old man ran from the house to the gate when Stevens and his party arrived and was the first one to whom Anderson spoke.

The old slave had heard the word "free." He knew what it meant. Yet he could not understand that freedom was for him.

"Free?" he asked. "You mean you don't need me? I can go back to my bed?"

"We are trying to tell you, man," Green said. "We come to free you from being slaves. All of you. Captain Smith is our leader, and Captain Stevens here. All of us, we are fighting for you. Go tell the others."

The old man stood looking as the small party swept by him. He had seen Captain Isaac Smith, as John Brown was called. He had seen him in the house of Colonel Washington. The two white men had talked together as friends.

He turned and started back toward the house, following those who offered him deliverance, but not accepting the gift.

Going into the house and facing Colonel Washington, Stevens and his men found him shaking with fear. He begged them not to kill him.

Stevens said, "You are our prisoner."

Stevens told him that they had come to free slaves and not to take life. He ordered Washington to get ready to go to Harpers Ferry.

The Colonel replied, "You can have my slaves if you will let me remain."

"No. You must go along too. Get ready," said Stevens.

For transport Stevens ordered some of the slaves, now liberated, to bring horses and a wagon.

Stevens demanded the surrender of Colonel Washington's arms. The Colonel owned a beautiful sword which had been presented to George Washington by Frederick the Great of Prussia at the close of the Revolutionary War. This was a great treasure. He pleaded that the sword not be surrendered. Stevens insisted that this was a fair trophy of the service. Washington brought it forth with tears in his eyes and offered it quite formally to Stevens.

Stevens stepped back and said, "You will present the sword to Mr. Anderson."

This was a special affront to Colonel Washington, slave owner. It was humiliating for him to present his prized trophy of war to a black man. Anderson accepted the sword. He went out of the house to the back porch.

Holding up the sword like an emblem of authority, he made a talk to the slaves who gathered around him.

"You are free," he said again. "We have come to fight, to make all the slaves free—we have guns. We have strong leaders and now we must make a great army of free men, of black men fighting to make other black men free."

He told them that Harpers Ferry had been captured.

They did not question him at first, but like the old man, they could not understand.

They were slaves.

They had never known life other than that of slaves. They had never been allowed to act or to think as free men and women. They had never been allowed to do or to say what they wanted to do or say. They had never been allowed to own anything of value.

All their lives they were told that they were property.

They had come to believe it.

They also believed that all white people were united in the system to keep black people as slaves.

A PREMATURE MOVEMENT.

JOHN BROWN. "Here! Take this, and follow me. My name's Brown."
CUFFEE. "Please God! Mr. Brown, dat is onpossible. We ain't done seedin' yit at our house."

It was impossible for most black slaves to believe that white men would lead in a fight against other white men in order to set black people free.

And this is why they could not fully understand or believe what they heard when Anderson and Green said, "You are free."

It was impossible for most of them to believe that white men would lead in a fight against other white men to make black men free.

A few believed. Some joined in the fight. And some died.

Stevens, with Colonel Washington his prisoner and with some of the Washington slaves as recruits, arrived at the armory.

All through Sunday night other prisoners were brought in. They were held in the engine house.

The engine house was really a fire-engine station. It was one of the buildings inside the walled area that was called the armory. The fire engine that was kept there was a hand-operated water pump mounted on wheels. Ladders and fire-fighting equipment were kept on another vehicle. The building had thick brick walls. Brown had already decided it could be used as a small fort.

People in the town were thoroughly frightened. No shots had been fired, but armed men, white and black, were taking in prisoners and others were taking up guard positions. Brown sent Lewis Leary with four slaves and a free black man to join Kagi and Copeland at the rifle works.

At about one o'clock in the morning the eastbound Baltimore and Ohio train arrived. It stopped at the Harpers Ferry station. The train crew saw some of the excited movement in the town, and they were told there was trouble.

A free black man, Hayward Shepherd by name, who was employed at the station, walked down the track toward the bridge. Two of Brown's men, Watson Brown and Stewart Taylor, seeing the man approach with his lantern, called upon him to halt. Shepherd did not stop. Instead he shouted a defiant word and turned to run away. He was shot. Within the hour he died.

Some people considered Shepherd a hero. The United Daughters of the Confederacy erected a monument to

John Brown seized the engine house in Harpers Ferry to use as a fort.

Hayward Shepherd at the site. The bronze tablet refers to his character and the faithfulness of thousands of Negroes who brought honor rather than disgrace upon themselves by refusing to share in the movement toward freedom.

The monument refers to Shepherd as a respected colored freeman. Actually, Shepherd was respected. Perhaps he was indeed a free man. But, legally he was the property of the mayor of the town, Fontaine Beckham, who also was killed in the fighting on October 17.

Since the telegraph wires had been cut, there was no communication between Harpers Ferry and the capital at Washington, D.C. However, on John Brown's order the train was allowed to proceed. Those at Harpers Ferry knew that the alarm to the country would be delivered.

13

Some Die, Some Escape, Some Are Captured, Nobody Surrenders

And so dawn came. The John Brown partisans held the rifle works, the arsenal, and the armory. They had taken some of the most prominent citizens of the area as prisoners, and they were holding them as hostages. Kagi and Copeland, with Leary and Leeman, along with some of the freed slaves, were in charge of the rifle works.

Have you guessed John Brown's next move?

Many people have tried to guess what Brown planned to do, and they have wondered why he did not take one of several steps that might have saved him and some of his men, advanced his struggle to free slaves, and delayed his capture and the collapse of his action.

He could have assembled the escaped slaves, his own men, and the hostages and retreated back across the Potomac River bridge. There on the Maryland side he could have gone into the hills, taking with him the supplies brought down from the farm. He might still have kept open the road to the farm and on into Chambersburg. This would not have been a very good plan because there were few slaves in Maryland and he would have cut himself off from the route down into the South where most of the slaves were.

He could have moved with his men, and with the slaves who were willing to fight, southward across the Shenandoah River. He could have taken his prisoners with him. Those who pursued him later would not have fought too hard for fear of harming the hostages. Also, he could have left a fairly strong party at Harpers Ferry to hold back his enemies. With this plan he could have moved the supplies from the schoolhouse and from the farm. Transportation was not too much of a problem, for just as he had taken a wagon and a team of horses from Colonel Washington's farm, he could have seized many more if he had had enough men.

Or he could have given up the fight. He had plenty of time to get his people together, cross the Potomac back into Maryland, and hurry back up the road to the farm and northward into Pennsylvania.

Finally, he could have used the hostages to bargain for terms of surrender.

Why did he do none of these?

In the morning Brown sent Tidd, Leeman, Cook, and fourteen newly released slaves back to the Kennedy farm. They went with the wagon that had been brought from Colonel Washington's farm. Their instructions were to secure and bring back the arms and ammunition that were stored at the farm. While it was only a five-mile trip, the terrain, the hills, the fords, and perhaps the muddy conditions of the roads made the trip a long one. It is not clear why the men took as long as they did. They brought one load of supplies down to the schoolhouse on the Maryland side of the Potomac River. They went back for a second load. When they came again it was too late. Had they returned earlier, these seventeen men with plenty of guns and ammunition might have saved John Brown and his party who were inside the walls of the armory.

Some of the people of the town may have wanted to see slavery abolished. However, most of them felt their sympathies were with the established government. Many of the men were employed in the rifle works or in the armory. Local citizens rallied with their own guns. A few of them had Sharps rifles. Some had guns made at the rifle works. They tried to organize an attack. Messengers were sent to Charlestown, others to Shepherdstown, and along the railway lines runners went out to warn oncoming trains. By nine o'clock in the morning companies of local militiamen were being assembled.

Those who later wrote about the event said that there developed, in the excitement, a tendency to make a carnival atmosphere out of the whole thing. There was a great deal of liquor drinking, of swaggering and shooting of six-guns in the air with no particular purpose except to say, "Look what we are doing."

To some extent John Brown and his men could feel themselves secure. However, they did know that the alarm was being spread and that counteraction would be taken. One company, the Jefferson Guards, approached on the Maryland side and seized the bridge; a company of Virginians took the bridge across the Shenandoah. Brown's only means of escape back to Mary-

Companies of militia and local guardsmen en route for Harpers Ferry after John Brown's attack.

land was now blocked. A small unit took possession of houses and shops facing the armory. At about noon the guardsmen on the Maryland side decided to attack. Brown saw them moving across the bridge.

By this time he had buckled on the great sword that had been taken from Colonel Washington. He used it until he was captured on the following day. It was a symbol of power, the badge of the commanding officer.

Brown ordered his men outside the walls of the armory and told them to prepare to defend themselves. Here is the story as reported by Osborn Anderson:

> Captain Brown said, "The troops are on the bridge, coming into town; we will give them a warm reception."
>
> He then walked around amongst us, giving us words of encouragement; then: "Be cool: Don't waste your powder and shot: Take aim, and make every shot count: The troops will look for us to retreat on their first appearance; be careful to shoot first."
>
> The troops soon came out of the bridge, and up the street facing us, we occupying an irregular position. When they got within 60 or 70 yards, Captain Brown

said, "Let go upon them:" Which we did when several of them fell. Again and again the dose was repeated. There was now consternation among the troops. From marching in solid martial columns, they became scattered. Some hastened to seize upon and bear up the wounded and dying, several lay dead upon the ground. They seemed not to realize, at first, that we would fire upon them, but evidently expected that we would be driven out by them without firing. Captain Brown seemed fully to understand the matter, and hence, very properly and in our defense, undertook to forestall their movements. . . . On the retreat of the troops, we were ordered back to our former post.

During this attack, Dangerfield Newby was killed, and his assailant was shot in turn by Shields Green. Two slaves also died fighting.

Things were going badly at the rifle works. Kagi sent word to John Brown suggesting that they should by all means withdraw. Brown replied that he would hold on a little longer. It is possible that he was hoping that the party from the farm would come back and drive off those who were on the Potomac side of the bridge.

Later Kagi sent word a second time urging that Brown give the order to withdraw. Again, the message was sent back that they would "wait a few minutes."

Jerry Anderson was the messenger. As he started back to the rifle works he was shot. He crawled back to the shelter of the engine house. Then shooting started at the rifle works, coming from all directions. The only possible avenue of escape was across the Shenandoah River, low at this season. Kagi and his companions tried this route. All the members of this party except Copeland were killed, either inside the rifle works or in their effort to get away. Copeland was captured in the river, unable to fire his gun because his powder was wet.

Brown must have realized that he was surrounded and there was little hope that reinforcements could get through to him. He had with him in the armory Colonel Washington and more than thirty other local citizens who had been captured. He thought he might negotiate. Under a flag of truce he sent William Thompson and one of his prisoners out with his offer: to release the prisoners in exchange for permission to withdraw. In the street Thompson was immediately seized. He was taken to the hotel.

We have an eyewitness report from one of the citizens, Henry Turner:

> We ducked into the room where he [William Thompson] was, and found several around him, but they offered only a feeble resistance; we brought our guns down to his head repeatedly, myself and other persons, for the purpose of shooting him in the room.
>
> There was a young lady there, the sister of Mr. Fouke, the hotel keeper, who sat in this man's lap, covered his face with her arms and shielded him with her person whenever we brought our guns to bear. She said to us, "For God's sake, wait and let the law take its course.". . . I was cool about it and deliberate. My gun was pushed by someone who seized the barrel, and I then moved to the back part of the room, still with purpose unchanged, but with a view to divert attention from me in order to get enough opportunity, at some moment when the crowd would be less dense, to shoot him. After a moment's thought, it occurred to me that that was not the proper place to kill him. We then proposed to take him out and hang him. Some

portion of our band then opened a way to him and first, pushing Miss Fouke aside, we slung him out-of-doors. I gave him a push and then the others did the same. We then shoved him along the platform and down to the press-work of the bridge; he begged for his life all the time, very piteously at first.

They shot him there, not once but many times. His body, hanging in the trestle work of the bridge for the rest of the afternoon, was a target for people who considered themselves sharpshooters. Then it fell into the water where it lay for the next two days.

The armory was under attack by militiamen and local citizens. The engine house, where Brown's men were holding the attackers off, was like a small fort. Oliver Brown was shot and he died without a word. Stewart Taylor was critically wounded.

Walking among the people of the town was Fontaine Beckham, the mayor, who kept trying to see what was happening. Once one of Brown's men started to fire, but John Brown called out, "Don't shoot. That man is not armed." Later in the day Edwin Coppoc saw Beckham and thought he was trying to approach to shoot. Coppoc fired, missed, and fired a second time, and Mayor Beckham slumped to the ground.

Prisoners in the engine house urged Brown to try to make terms with the citizens. They suggested that Brown and his men, those still living, might be allowed to escape. Brown did consider such an act. He sent out his son Watson and Stevens, one of the prisoners, with a white flag, but the angry and drunken crowd did not honor it. Watson was shot down as soon as he started out but he managed to get back. Stevens, badly wounded, was taken to the railway station.

Before dark Brown selected eleven of the prisoners in the armory and secured them inside the engine house. To the eleven he said, "Gentlemen, perhaps you wonder why I have selected you from the others. It is because I believe you to be the most influential, and I have only to say now, that you will have precisely the same fate that your friends extend to my men."

Among the prominent prisoners was John E. Daingerfield. He later gave an eyewitness account which was published in the June 1885 issue of *Century Magazine*. About John Brown he wrote:

> I found him as brave as a man could be, and sensible upon all subjects except slavery. He believed it was his duty to free the slaves, even if in doing so he lost his own life. During a sharp fight one of Brown's sons [Oliver] was killed. He fell; then trying to raise himself he said, "It is all over with me," and died instantly. Brown did not leave his post at the porthole; but when the fighting was over he walked to his son's body, straightened out his limbs, took off his trappings, and then turning to me, said, "This is the third son I have lost in this cause." Another son [Watson] had been shot in the morning and was then dying, having been brought in from the street. Often during the affair at the engine house, when his men would want to fire upon someone who might be seen passing, Brown would stop, saying, "Don't shoot; that man is unarmed."

Brown called most of his men from their stations around the walls. They proceeded to knock out holes in the bricks as portholes for their guns. Albert Hazlett,

Osborn Anderson, and Shields Green were the only ones left to guard the armory walls. Green was not happy at his post. He told Hazlett that he wanted to be inside the engine house with Brown. Hazlett agreed to let him go. Another wave of attack came from the outside. The gates of the armory were smashed in, and those prisoners who had not been taken into the engine house were released. Anderson and Hazlett thought that the battle was lost. The two of them went over the back wall and made their escape.

More volunteers and militiamen were coming in from nearby places. They came from Winchester, Virginia, and from Baltimore, Maryland. The town assumed a military appearance. In the nation's capital President James Buchanan was told that a party of seven hundred insurrectionists, blacks and whites, had captured the town of Harpers Ferry with all its military supplies. He ordered out three companies of artillery and one company of marines.

By train Colonel Robert E. Lee, with 100 marines, arrived just before midnight. This is the same Robert E. Lee who later became famous as the commanding general of the Confederate forces during the Civil War. Colonel Lee's second in command was Lieutenant J.E.B. Stuart. He also became famous as a general in the southern army.

Colonel Lee sent Stuart under a flag of truce to the engine house. Brown's forces held their fire. They admitted the officer. As Stuart approached, a light was brought and the officer recognized Brown.

"Why, aren't you Osawatomie Brown of Kansas, whom I once had there as my prisoner?" he demanded.

"Yes," John Brown replied, "but you did not keep me."

In answer to a demand that he surrender and trust to the clemency of the government, John Brown said, "I prefer to die here."

Lieutenant Stuart withdrew.

Just after daylight, Lieutenant Stuart called out again demanding surrender, and from Brown he had the same answer, "I prefer to die here."

The door was attacked with sledgehammers. It did not yield. The soldiers brought a ladder to be used as a battering ram. The door gave in. An officer and some of his men rushed in. The lieutenant, Israel Green, swung with his sword, striking Brown about midway in the body; witnesses said the blow raised Brown's body from the ground. Brown fell back and Green struck several more times. It is said that the sword bent double. John Brown, his wounded son Watson, Shields Green, and Edwin Coppoc were captured in the engine house.

Oliver Brown, Dauphin and William Thompson, John Kagi, Stewart Taylor, Dangerfield Newby, Lewis Leary, Watson Brown, and Jerry Anderson were fatally wounded—ten in all—in the fight for Harpers Ferry. The number of slaves who were killed is not known.

Copeland was captured in the river near the rifle works. Cook, who had gone up to the farm, was captured later, as was Hazlett, who had escaped during the fighting.

Six others—Owen Brown, Tidd, Leeman, Barclay Coppoc, Meriam, and Osborn Anderson—escaped.

14

Slaves Can't Trust Anybody

Osborn Anderson has described in detail the events of his escape with Captain Hazlett. When the militiamen broke into the armory grounds, Anderson and Hazlett escaped by going over the wall. They ran crouched along the bank of the Shenandoah River. They crossed the peninsula above the town and came down on the Potomac side. Here they found a rowboat, which they used to cross the Potomac. Soldiers and volunteers were out seeking those who might have escaped. In the night Hazlett and Anderson were fired upon. They took refuge in the rocky bluffs by the river. They looked down on soldiers who were firing at them, but those on the road below were fearful of going into the hills. Anderson reports also that they saw slaves with guns, but they could not get close enough to talk to these black men.

At one time four, or perhaps five, slaves passed near the place where they were hiding. Anderson called to them.

"Hey. Come over here," he said. "We are friends."

The others ran away. He could hear them across the rocks and through the brush.

"We're your friends," Hazlett shouted. "Wait for us."

Again and again they tried to make contact. It was always the same.

Hazlett said bitterly, "They don't trust us."

"They don't trust anybody," Anderson replied. "They can't trust anybody. They're slaves."

"But if I was a slave I'd be ready to trust anybody to fight for my freedom."

"That's what you think, but you're wrong. No man born free and grown up free can know how it feels to be a slave. And more, no white man can know how it feels to be black, slave or free. Do you remember the old man up at Colonel Washington's big gate? He couldn't understand. He can't know what the word 'free' means. He probably can't even dream about it."

Anderson tried to explain that slaves lived their whole lives in fear, not daring to trust anyone. Owners maintained their controls without legal or moral restraint, and slaves were convinced that all white people were the same. They could not believe that any white man would fight to free black slaves, and they could not trust the bearded white man whom they had seen going in and out of the homes of their masters.

On the Maryland side of the Potomac the two men made their way up to the farm. It was deserted. They came down the road again to the schoolhouse, arriving at about two o'clock in the morning. They knew that searchers would be there, so they did not stop but made their way up into the hills again to rest. In the night they woke up to the sounds of gunfire, and they could see soldiers firing into the hills. Some of the escaping slaves fired back at the soldiers.

With daylight Anderson and Hazlett started northward, hoping to reach Chambersburg. Ten miles south of that small city the two men parted. Hazlett was at the point of exhaustion. It was also obvious that a white man and a black man moving together through the country were especially subject to attack.

While at Chambersburg searchers came to the house where Anderson was hiding. He went out the back door and made his getaway. Going on that night, sleeping in a haystack the next day, he walked until he reached York, Pennsylvania. In the night he found a friend and help. Later he took a train from York to Philadelphia, and went on to Canada.

Hazlett was less fortunate. He succeeded in reaching Chambersburg, but he was fearful, he did not stop there. Federal officers were close behind him. He was arrested in Pennsylvania and returned to Virginia.

Owen Brown and the others who had been at the Kennedy farm trying to transfer the supplies down to Harpers Ferry moved northward. They were hunted men. At times they saw soldiers and citizens looking for them. They had no food. Their clothes were torn to tatters. Their feet were practically bare. It took them fourteen days to reach Chambersburg. Meriam at that time was sick and lame. Cook was frantic in his hunger. He wanted to approach farmers in the area or go into one of the towns to secure food. The others cautioned him against it. Cook and Tidd were involved in an argument and would have fought over this issue had the others not stopped them. Cook said he had to have salt pork, and he left the party in the mountains to go into the town of Motaldo, fourteen miles from Chambersburg. He was captured there on October 26. Without being taken through formalities of extradition, Cook was taken from Pennsylvania back to Virginia and lodged in the Charlestown jail to be tried and executed.

The others went to Chambersburg but did not enter the town. They did, however, communicate with one friend there. Meriam received help, and he was put on a train to Philadelphia. From there he went to Boston and then to Canada. The other three went to Center County, Pennsylvania. Barclay Coppoc went to Canada, while Tidd and Owen Brown went to Ohio. The state of Virginia tried to have Tidd and Brown extradited but the governor of Ohio refused to cooperate in the criminal proceedings.

15

The Prisoner Tells His Story

On Tuesday morning, October 18, 1859, John Brown, alias Isaac Smith, also known as Old Osawatomie Brown, was taken from the engine house more dead than alive.

It took a troop of United States Marines and perhaps nine hundred militiamen and armed citizens finally to capture John Brown. It is remarkable that the old man survived the wounds of bayonet and saber.

John Brown and the wounded Stevens were taken to the main building of the armory. John Brown lay for eighteen hours on the floor of the paymaster's office. Green, Edwin Coppoc, and Watson Brown were locked in another room which was heavily guarded.

Coppoc wrote to Mrs. Brown in New York. A passage from the letter is given here:

> I was with your sons when they fell. Oliver lived but a few minutes after he was shot. He spoke no word but yielded calmly to his fate. Watson was shot at 10:00 on Monday morning and died about 3:00 Wednesday morning. He suffered much. Though mortally

John Brown, wounded, lay on the ground while U.S. Marines brought out from the engine house the men held hostage by Brown's raiders.

wounded at 10:00, yet at 3:00 Monday afternoon he fought bravely against the men who charged on us. When the enemy were repulsed, and the excitement of the charge was over, he began to sink rapidly. After we were taken prisoners, he was placed in the guard house with me. He complained of the hardness of the bench on which he was lying. I begged hard for a bed for him, or even a blanket, but could obtain none for him. I took off my coat and placed it under him, and held his head in my lap, in which position he died, without a groan or struggle.

According to Joseph Barry, a schoolteacher who wrote a book called *The Strange Story of Harpers Ferry*, Jeremiah Anderson was "dragged out of the engine house to the flagged walk in front; he was yet alive and vomiting gore from internal hemorrhage."

After he died, some physicians of Winchester, Virginia, took his body, according to the same writer. They packed it into a barrel.

> Head foremost they rammed him in, but they could not bend his legs so as to get them into the barrel with the rest of his body. In their endeavors to accomplish this feat, the man's bones, or sinuses, fairly cracked. The praiseworthy exertions of these sons of Galan, in the cause of science and humanity, elicited the warmest expressions of approval from the spectators. The writer does not know what disposition was finally made of him.

We do know that the body of Oliver Brown was thrown into a shallow grave with that of Dangerfield Newby. The body of his brother Watson was taken to the medical college at Winchester where it was put on exhibit. In 1862 after that area of Virginia was controlled by the Union army, the body was rescued by an army surgeon. It was buried in Virginia. Many years later the remains of both Oliver and Watson were removed and taken to North Elba. They were buried in the plot near the grave of their father.

Barry was also witness to events that occurred around Dangerfield Newby. Newby was the free man whose wife was a slave and mother of his children. Immediately after the affair at Harpers Ferry, she was sold to a trader of Louisiana. Barry's story follows:

> Shortly after Newby's death a hog came up, rooted around the spot where the body lay and at first appeared to be unconscious that anything extraordinary

was in its way. After a while the hog paused and looked attentively at the body, then sniffed around it and put its snout to the dead man's face. Suddenly the brute was apparently seized with a panic, and, with bristles erect and drooping tail, it scampered away as if for dear life. This display of sensibility did not, however, deter others of the same species from crowding around the corpse and almost literally devouring it. The writer saw all this with his own eyes, as the saying is, and, at the risk of further criticism, he will remark that none of the good people of Harpers Ferry appeared to be at all squeamish about the quality of flavor of their pork that winter. Nobody thought about the subject, or, if anybody did recall the episode it was no doubt, to give credit to the hogs for their rough treatment of the invaders.

On Tuesday evening, after Brown's capture, and when the people were somewhat relieved from the terror of a more extensive and dangerous invasion, a citizen of Harpers Ferry who had not had a chance to distinguish himself in the skirmish of Monday, fired a shot into what was left of Newby's body. A feat which, it must be supposed, tended to exalt him, at least, in his own estimation.

Soldiers were sent to round up the fugitives, but most of them made good their escape. Some of the soldiers went to the Kennedy farm and to the schoolhouse where they took possession of the arms and the personal properties of Brown and his men. The small wagon and the mule were confiscated. They were seized by Fouke, the hotel keeper, to pay for meals that Brown had ordered to feed his prisoners.

The military supplies that were captured included 180

Sharps rifles and 75 Allen revolvers. Also, 950 pikes were taken. There were other supplies—powder, caps, and lead for making additional rifle balls.

Governor Henry A. Wise of Virginia arrived from Richmond in the afternoon of October 18th by train. On the same train came many other officials and a host of newsmen and reporters. One of the newsmen was a man who called himself Porte Crayon, an artist for *Frank Leslie's Illustrated Newspaper*. His strong line drawings describing the scenes, and later those of the execution of John Brown, were published in Leslie's weekly and circulated throughout the world.

With the governor were Senator James M. Mason of Virginia, author of one of the fugitive slave laws, and Congressman Clement L. Vallandigham of Ohio. They questioned Brown as he lay on the floor, unattended for his wounds, unfed, unwashed. Reporters were present and they took down the conversation. The dialogue was published in the *New York Herald*. Perhaps never before had an interview had such wide-felt effects.

John Brown's revolver and pike.

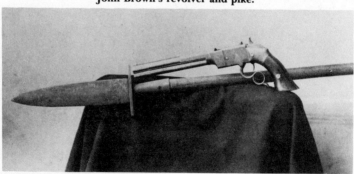

Mason asked, "Can you tell us who furnished money for your expedition?"

"I furnished most of it myself," Brown replied. "I cannot implicate others. It is by my own folly that I have been taken. I could easily have saved myself from it, if I had exercised my own better judgment rather than yielding to my feelings. I should have gone away, but I had thirty-odd prisoners, whose wives and daughters were in tears for their safety, and I felt for them. Besides, I wanted to allay the fears of those who believe we came here to burn and kill. For this reason I allowed the train to cross the bridge, and gave them full liberty to pass on. I did it only to spare the feelings of those passengers and their families, and to allay the apprehensions that you had got here in your vicinity a band of men who had no regard for life and property, nor any feelings of humanity."

Congressman Vallandigham wanted to know about activities in Ohio and especially whether any of Brown's men had come from that state. Brown answered honestly but he would give no names.

Vallandigham asked, "Did you get up the expedition yourself?"

"I did," Brown replied.

"How long have you been engaged in this business?"

"From the breaking out of the difficulties in Kansas. Four of my sons had gone there to settle, and they induced me to go. I did not go to settle, but because of the difficulties."

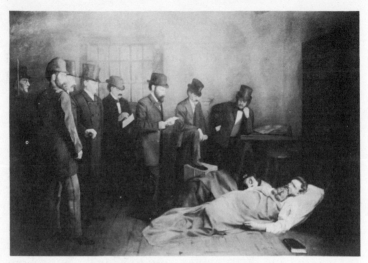

The wounded John Brown is questioned.
Next to Brown lies Aaron Stevens.

"Did you go to Kansas under auspices of the Emigrant Aid Society?"

"No, sir, I went under auspices of John Brown, and nobody else."

In answering other questions Brown said that he did indeed believe that he was an instrument in the hands of Providence and that he justified his action on the Golden Rule. The reporters observed his weak condition. One of them finally said that if he wished to make a final statement it would be duly reported.

Brown lifted himself and tried to summarize. He gave a prophetic warning.

"I wish to say, furthermore, that you had better—all you people of the South—prepare yourselves for a settlement of this question. It must come up for settlement sooner than you are prepared for it. The sooner you are prepared for it, the better.

"You may dispose of me very easily. I am nearly disposed of now; but this question is still to be settled, this Negro question, I mean. The end of that is not yet."

Someone shouted from the crowd, "I think you are fanatical."

Brown replied, "And I think you are fanatical. 'Whom the gods would destroy, they first make mad,' and you are mad."

For thirty hours John Brown was in that guarded building. Then he and his companions Green, Stevens, and Edwin Coppoc were taken to the jail at Charlestown, the seat of Jefferson County. There he was to await trial in a Virginia court, only one week after his capture.

John Brown has been described as a fanatic and a madman. Two of the persons who were at this scene, several others who were in court during the trial, and many others who were in touch with him thought otherwise.

Mr. Vallandigham returned to Ohio and there he testified as follows:

> It is vain to underrate either the man or the conspiracy. Captain John Brown is as brave and resolute a man as ever headed an insurrection, and, in a good cause, and with sufficient force, would have been a consummate partisan commander. He had coolness, daring, persistency, stoic faith and patience, and a firmness of will and purpose unconquerable. He is the farthest possible removed from the ordinary ruffian, fanatic or

madman. Certainly it was one of the best executed con-
spiracies that ever failed.

Here also are the words of Henry A. Wise, governor
of Virginia:

> They are themselves mistaken who take him to be a
> madman. He is a bundle of the best nerves I ever saw,
> cut, and thrust, and bleeding and in bonds. He is a
> man of clear head, of courage, fortitude, and the simple
> ingenuousness. He is cool, collected, and indomitable,
> and it is but just to him to say that he was humane
> to his prisoners . . . and he inspired me with great
> trust in his integrity, as a man of truth.

16

"I Am Ready for My Fate"

On Thursday, October 20, 1859, John Brown and his companions were formally committed to jail in Charlestown. John Copeland was already locked up there.

The jail building was just at the back of the courthouse. Visitors to Charlestown will now see the county jail as part of the courthouse. At that time it was apart from the courthouse building. Brown and Aaron Stevens occupied one cell; Stevens, as well as Brown, was badly wounded. Edwin Coppoc was in another cell. After his capture on October 26, John Cook was held in the cell with Coppoc. Green and Copeland, both black men, were in a third cell. Later, after his capture, Albert Hazlett was put in another cell, alone.

Governor Wise decided to prosecute Brown and the others in Virginia courts rather than allow federal authorities to take charge. The state courts could handle the whole case swiftly. A grand jury was in session in Jefferson County at the time, and Judge Richard Parker

A view of Charlestown, Virginia, showing the prison (far left), guardhouse (center), and courthouse (far right) where John Brown and his men were tried.

had just opened the semiannual session of the circuit court. Had there been a delay, a mob might have broken into the jail and lynched the prisoners without any trial. Also, it was thought that Stevens might die of his wounds before being declared guilty.

On Tuesday, October 25, one week after they were captured, the prisoners were given a preliminary hearing in magistrate's court. John Brown was taken into court with Edwin Coppoc, to whom he was chained. In the courtroom Brown was allowed to lie on a cot. Stevens, breathing with difficulty, was at first commanded to remain standing with Coppoc, Copeland, and Green. Later Stevens was allowed to lie on the floor.

The presiding justice, after the charges were read, ordered Brown to enter his plea. Instead of entering a plea of guilty or not guilty, Brown got to his feet and made a statement.

"Virginians," he said, "I did not ask for any quarter at the time I was taken. I did not ask to have my life spared. The governor of the State of Virginia tendered me assurances that I should have a fair trial. . . . If you seek my blood, you can have it at any time without this mockery of a trial. I have no counsel. I have not been able to advise with anyone. I know nothing about the feelings of my fellow prisoners, and am utterly unable to attend in any way to my own defense. . . . There are mitigating circumstances that I would urge, if a fair trial is to be had. But if we are forced with a mere form— a trial for execution—you might spare yourselves that trouble. I am ready for my fate. I beg for no mockery of a trial—no insult—nothing but that which conscience gives or cowardice would drive you to practice. . . . I have now little further to ask other than I may not be foolishly insulted, as only cowardly barbarians insult those who fall into their power."

Two local lawyers, Lawson Botts and Thomas C. Green, were assigned by the court as defense counsel. Green was at that time mayor of Charlestown. Brown said that he had sent a message north requesting his own counsel. He did not at any time acknowledge these court-appointed lawyers as counsel for himself. The other prisoners did accept them.

On the following day, Wednesday, the 26th, the grand jury returned indictments alleging for each of the prisoners slave conspiracy, murder, robbery, and treason.

Trial was set for the following day, Thursday.

The town of Charlestown looked like a military post. Soldiers with fixed bayonets were everywhere. Hundreds of state troopers were encamped about the town. Two cannons were planted to cover the courthouse grounds. The railway station at Harpers Ferry, the only entrance to that area by rail, was also heavily guarded.

The formal trial started eleven days after the raid on Harpers Ferry. It is clear that the prosecution, led by Andrew Hunter as the state's attorney, hoped to have John Brown tried, convicted, and executed without delay. It is equally clear that although John Brown knew he would be executed, he wanted to have an open trial in order that his statements could be made public. He wanted to speak to the world with the help of reporters present and with the help of the official records of the court. He wanted to warn the nation of the perilous course on which it was headed.

Hunter was the central figure of the prosecution.

Colonel Lewis Washington was a conspicuous witness. He looked much like his great-uncle George Washington.

A comic relief was provided by the person of a Colonel J. Lewis Davis, a strange-looking dignitary. He wore his hair in two braids tied together by a bow over his forehead. All through the trial he carried one of the rifles looted from John Brown's stock. He seemed especially anxious to harass the newspapermen. On his order one of them was driven out of town.

Through the several days of the court proceedings John Brown, at each session, was allowed to lie on a cot.

On the first day court-appointed Attorney Lawson Botts presented a dispatch sent from Cleveland, Ohio. It alleged that Captain Brown was insane. The document was originated by friends of Brown and one relative, Jeremiah Brown, a half-brother.

Brown objected to any such consideration. He struggled up from his cot to make his own speech. He concluded with these words: "I will add, if the court will allow me, that I look upon it as a miserable artifice and trick of those who ought to take a different course in regard to me, if it took any at all, and I view it with contempt more than otherwise. . . . I am perfectly unconscious of insanity, and I reject so far as I am capable any attempts to interfere in my behalf on that score."

From then on John Brown seemed to be quite cooperative with the court. He made no denials of certain of the facts that were presented. He identified, as they were handed to him, all the documents, papers, items found at the Kennedy farmhouse, or at the schoolhouse.

John Brown had indeed sent to his friends in the North requesting counsel. It is not certain that his messages arrived, but newspapers helped to get the word to friends in New York and New England. George Henry Hoyt came down from Massachusetts. He was very young and had, therefore, little experience. However, he was brave, quick-witted, and keen.

Hoyt arrived on Thursday. The young lawyer was not allowed to see the prisoners, but on Friday morning

The trial of John Brown at Charlestown, Virginia. The wounded

John Brown was allowed to lie on a cot during court proceedings.

he did appear in court. On Friday afternoon, when it appeared that the case was about to be closed, John Brown got Hoyt's attention, and pointed to a piece of paper lying on the floor near Shields Green. Hoyt picked up the paper and read it, then rose to his feet and read it to the court.

It had been written by Brown. It said: "May it please the court, I discovered that, notwithstanding all the assertions I have received of a fair trial, nothing like a fair trial is to be given me, as it would seem. I gave the names as soon as I could get at them of the persons I wish to have called as witnesses, and was assured they would be subpoenaed. I wrote down a memorandum to that effect saying where those parties were, but it appears that they have not been subpoenaed, so far as I can learn, and I now ask if I am to have anything at all deserving the name and shadow of a fair trial, that this proceeding be deferred until tomorrow morning. . . ."

The document went on to say that he wanted his witnesses. He said he had no one to do errands for him. He was without funds, although at the time of his capture he had $250 taken from his person.

This charge of failure on the part of his lawyers, who were supposedly representing him, threw the court into consternation. Botts and Green asked for a recess. It was granted. Botts and Green withdrew from the case, and Hoyt was left in charge. Hoyt's request for delay was denied, but he was allowed to speak.

He spoke with great force and deep passion. He was as earnest in his antagonism to slavery as was John Brown himself. His words brought about his dismissal by the judge, who required him to leave the state under the prodding of Colonel J. Lewis Davis. However, on the grounds that further witnesses were to be called, the court was recessed until the following morning. To this next session Samuel Chilton of Washington and Hiram Griswold of Cleveland came to speak for Brown.

Both men were mature and experienced lawyers. Mr. Chilton, a Virginian, was connected with some prominent families. He was thoroughly familiar with the laws of the state, the court practices, and the feelings of the people.

Chilton and Griswold requested a delay in order that they might acquaint themselves with the papers, the full story, and the defendants themselves. Judge Parker denied the motion, saying, "The trial must proceed."

The case went to the jury on Monday after almost six hours of arguments by defense counsels Chilton and Griswold and by the state's attorney for the prosecution, Hunter. In approximately one hour the jury returned with a verdict of guilty.

For a while no one spoke.

John Brown raised himself on his cot. He straightened the folded blanket under his head. He lay back down without any show of emotion.

Everyone present seemed to feel the tragedy of this situation.

Counsel Chilton entered a motion for arrest of judgment. Without making a decision the judge recessed the trial of Brown until the next day, when closing arguments would be heard.

Edwin Coppoc was called to the bar and his trial proceeded for less than two days.

On the second day of November, while the jury was out on the Coppoc matter, John Brown was brought back into court. He walked with difficulty. His face showed an expression of firm composure, but it was twisted with the pain of his movement. He took a place in a chair beside his counsels. The judge overruled the exceptions of counsels.

"Does the defendant have any reason why sentence should not be passed upon him?" asked the clerk of the court.

John Brown rose slowly to his feet. He put his hands on the table in front of him. Leaning slightly forward, in a voice that was quiet and self-controlled, and in gentle tones, he made this speech:

"I have, may it please the court, a few words to say: In the first place, I deny everything but what I have all along admitted,—the designs on my part to free the slaves. I intended certainly to have made a clean thing of the matter, as I did last winter, when I went to Missouri and took slaves without the snapping of a gun on either side, moved them through the country, and finally left them in Canada. I designed to have done the same thing again, on a larger scale. That was all I intended. I never did intend murder, treason, or the destruction of property, or to excite slaves to rebellion, or to make insurrection.

"I have another objection: and that is, it is unjust that I should suffer such a penalty. Had I interfered in the manner which I admit, and which I admit has been fairly proved (for I admire the truthfulness and candor of the greater portion of the witnesses who have testified in this case), had I so interfered in behalf of the rich, the powerful, the intelligent, the so-called great, or in behalf of any of their friends—either father, mother, brother, sister, wife or children, or any of that class—and suffered and sacrificed what I have in this interference, it would have been all right; and every man in this court would have deemed it an act worthy of reward rather than punishment.

"This court acknowledges, as I suppose, the validity of the law of God. I see a book kissed here which I suppose is the Bible, or at least the New Testament. That teaches me that whatsoever I would that men should do to me, I should do even so to them. It teaches me further to 'remember them that are in bonds, as bound with them.' I endeavored to act up to that instruction. I say, I am yet too young to understand that God is any respecter of persons. I believe that to have interfered as I have done—as I have always freely admitted I have done—in behalf of His despised poor, was not wrong, but right. Now, if it is deemed necessary that I should forfeit my life for the furtherance of the ends of justice, and mingle my blood further with the blood of my children and with the blood of millions in this slave country whose rights are disregarded by wicked, cruel, and unjust enactments—I submit; so let it be done.

"Let me say one word further.

"I feel entirely satisfied with the treatment I have received on my trial. Considering all the circumstances, it has been more generous than I expected. But I feel no consciousness of guilt. I have stated from the first what was my intention, and what was not. I never had any design against the life of any person, nor any disposition to commit treason, or excite slaves to rebel, or make

any general insurrection. I never encouraged any man
to do so, but always discouraged any idea of the kind.

"Let me say, also a word in regard to the statements
made by some of those connected with me. I hear it
has been stated by some of them that I have induced
them to join me. But the contrary is true. I do not say
this to injure them, but as regarding their weakness.
There is not one of them but joined me of his own
accord, and the greater part of them at their own ex-
pense. A number of them I never saw, and never had
a word of conversation with, till the day they came to
me; and that was for the purpose I have stated. Now,
I have done!"

People across the country read Brown's speech as set
down in shorthand by reporters and published in newspapers. Some years later Ralph Waldo Emerson com-
pared it in quality to Lincoln's Gettysburg Address.

Judge Parker was not impressed. He sentenced John
Brown to death by hanging on the gallows in Jefferson
County, Virginia, on December 2, 1859.

17

Companions Convicted

Companions of John Brown were also tried.

Edwin Coppoc was convicted on November 2.

Shields Green and John Copeland were tried and convicted in two days. Green, who had spent most of his life in slavery, was without education. He was blunt and perhaps stubborn, but at times he showed fierce emotion. Copeland had always been free, and he was fairly well educated. He spoke clearly and calmly, making a good showing in court.

Another young lawyer, George Sennott, came down from Boston to help. He argued that because black people had been deprived of citizenship by the Supreme Court's Dred Scott decision, no Negro could be guilty of treason against Virginia. He further said that these two black men were justified in resisting enslavement of members of their race. The prosecution agreed with the argument regarding treason, but the jury found both men guilty of murder and conspiring with slaves to rebel.

John Cook was perhaps in the most perilous position of all those present. One writer has said that the community would rather have seen John Brown go free than to have permitted Cook to live. Cook had come into the area, married a local girl, and ingratiated himself to the leading people of Harpers Ferry and the area around it. While selling his books and his maps, while asking questions and making sketches of the area, he had gained complete knowledge of the country and its people.

Cook had influential relatives. His brother-in-law was A. P. Willard, governor of Indiana. The governor and two Indiana lawyers appeared in court to help Cook. In spite of this expert help Cook was convicted on November 9.

On November 10 the four convicted men were in court for sentence. The two black men refused to speak, but Coppoc and Cook insisted that they had not been aware of John Brown's real plan until a few hours before the attack. They expected to be punished for what they had done but, they said, they ought not be put to death.

The judge did not agree. He sentenced the four convicted men to death by hanging on December 16, 1859.

The trials had been before Virginia judges under the laws of Virginia, but Governor Wise ordered that Aaron Stevens be held for trial in federal court. The governor wanted to be sure that the federal government should have continuing interest. The United States was sharing responsibility and also expenses.

On November 5 Albert Hazlett was brought to Charlestown from Pennsylvania where he had been arrested after getting that far with Osborn Anderson. Haz-

**Shields Green, John Copeland, and Albert Hazlett
in the Charlestown jail.**

lett insisted that he was a victim of mistaken identity. He said he was William H. Harrison. The district court adjourned on November 10, 1859, leaving the matter of Albert Hazlett, alias William H. Harrison, for the next term, to begin in February 1860.

Stevens and Hazlett were both brought to trial at the next session of the circuit court. Sennott challenged the court's jurisdiction over Stevens because Governor Wise had supposedly given him over to the federal government. Sennott also stressed the lack of convincing proof that "William H. Harrison" was indeed one of those who had taken part in the Harpers Ferry raid. However, both men were found guilty. They were sentenced to hang on March 16, 1860.

18

"Good-bye, Good-bye . . . God Bless You"

The word went out.

From Harpers Ferry and from Charlestown, the message of John Brown, his Cry for Freedom, went out. It went not only to the northern cities; it went into the Deep South where slavery was firmly entrenched.

Newspapermen from the *New York Herald* wrote long accounts of the events. They reported in detail interviews with John Brown and others. Of course, the reporters had no electronic recording devices, but they took down the speeches and testimony and conversations in shorthand. The *New York Herald* and the *New York Tribune*, the *Baltimore American and Commercial Advertiser*, and even the *New Orleans Times-Democrat* carried stories of the procedures. The *Atlantic Monthly* published articles, as did the German language newspaper, *The New Yorker Demokrat*. Other magazines and weeklies had representatives present in Charlestown.

Of particular interest today is the work of *Frank Leslie's Illustrated Newspaper.* This was a popular news sheet of some sixteen to thirty-two pages. The pictures were made not from photographs but from on-the-scene line drawings. One of their artists was ordered out of Charlestown during the trial. However, he did return, and some of the most interesting drawings produced in connection with the execution of John Brown were made by him.

These newsmen, hardened by experience, devoid of emotion, trained in objective observation and recording, told the story of the events as they unfolded. They recorded and repeated John Brown's words.

"This is no madman," they said to everyone.

From his cell in Charlestown John Brown wrote no less than a dozen letters to his wife and other members of his family. He wrote more letters to his friends and supporters. Many of the letters are published in volumes on file in our libraries.

Newspapers carried the story of interviews with his wife and the story of Mrs. Brown's last visit with her husband while he awaited execution.

Mrs. Brown wrote to Governor Wise of Virginia asking that the body of her husband and the bodies of her sons Watson and Oliver be released to her. She received a courteous reply. She would be allowed to claim the body of John Brown immediately after his execution. The bodies of her sons were not available to the family until several years later.

A reporter asked Mrs. Brown about the possibility of a plea on the basis of her husband's being insane. She replied, "I couldn't say, if I were called upon, that my husband was insane—even to save his life, because he wasn't."

The reporter added that she spoke as if the utterance of an untruth were a natural as well as a moral impossibility to her.

On November 30 she arrived at Harpers Ferry in the company of two friends from Philadelphia. She was detained at Harpers Ferry. Military and court officials entered into a hasty conference. Finally, on the following day, a file of dragoons (a squad or troop of soldiers on horseback) was sent to escort her to Charlestown.

She arrived at the courthouse, with the jail building at the rear, at four o'clock in the afternoon. The carriage in which she rode was surrounded by twenty-five horsemen. The road, as they came in, was thronged with hundreds of eager spectators. Mrs. Brown left the carriage and moved up the steps between rows of rifles with bayonets fixed and rows of artillery.

Mrs. Avis, wife of the jailer, took Mrs. Brown into a private room and searched her for concealed weapons. As the jailer led her into the room to face her husband, it is said that she and John Brown stood for a moment speechless. And then she moved into his arms where he embraced her.

Neither of them spoke for a few minutes. After they were seated, John Brown spoke first. "Wife, I am glad to see you," he said.

"My dear husband, it is a hard fate," she answered.

"Well, well. Cheer up, cheer up, Mary," Brown told her. "We must all bear it in the best manner we can. I believe it is all for the best."

"Our poor children—God help them!"

"Those that are dead to this world are angels in another. How are all those still living? Tell them their father died without a single regret for the course he has pursued—that he is satisfied he is right in the eyes of God and of all just men."

They spoke of the living children and the grandchildren and of close friends of the family. He gave instructions with regard to business, and he read to her his will, carefully explaining every portion of it.

After this conversation they ate a final meal together. Mrs. Brown expressed the wish to see the other prisoners, but this privilege was denied. It was not long before the visit was terminated because it was necessary for her to be taken back, with the military escort, to Harpers Ferry. The officials wanted the trip to be made before dark.

John and Mary Brown's last meal together in the parlor of Mr. Avis, the jailer.

"Good-bye, good-bye," he said as he kissed her for the last time. "God bless you!"

Captain John Avis, the jailer, was a pleasant man, short of stature, perhaps of less than middle age, who proved to be a real friend to the men he held. He lived with his wife in the building. It was his duty to guard, protect, and feed the prisoners.

Sheriff James Campbell was also kindly disposed. He respected John Brown and, in turn, Brown and the other prisoners respected him.

Campbell and Avis were well aware of their responsibilities as the execution date, December 2, approached.

More than three thousand soldiers, militia, army, marines, and cavalrymen were stationed around the town. On December 1 a scaffold was erected in the center of a vacant field about a half-mile from the courthouse. The platform was six feet high, twelve feet wide, and about fifteen feet in length. A handrail extended around three sides and down the flight of steps. An iron hook was suspended from a crossbeam that was supported by two stout uprights.

The atmosphere was tense. Frightening reports were being circulated. There were rumors of slave insurrections and attempts by friends to release the prisoner. At eight o'clock in the morning soldiers marched onto the field. Infantrymen and cavalrymen formed a hollow square. A brass cannon was placed at the front, aimed directly toward the gallows. It was charged and loaded with grapeshot. Had anything gone amiss the cannon could have been fired, blowing the person at the gallows to bits. That others around it would have been harmed was obvious. Other artillery pieces were placed strate-

gically, some turned toward the jail, some aimed at every
approach. Five hundred soldiers were posted in this
square immediately around the scaffold. Before John
Brown was taken out of his cell the sheriff, the jailer,
and the assistants entered. They told Brown good-bye,
and Brown thanked them for their courtesies. He was
then taken to the cell of Shields Green and John Copeland. Next he bade farewell to John Cook and Edwin
Coppoc. At last he visited Aaron Stevens.

John Brown did not visit Albert Hazlett. Up to that
time Hazlett had denied his identity. Brown did not
embarrass him by claiming him as a friend and compan-
ion.

Details of these last hours were carefully reported in
the press. One of those who shared his experience was
a newsman who had gotten a job with the authorities.
He drove the wagon that took John Brown on his last
ride from the jail to the scaffold.

The prisoner left the jail corridor with his ankles
bound together by a short chain. His hands were chained
behind him. Armed guards were ahead of him and behind him. The sheriff was at his right side and the jailer
at his left.

Just outside the jailhouse door a slave woman stood
with her child in her arms. John Brown stopped in his
stride, leaned over, and kissed the black baby.

Another black woman called to him, "God bless you,
old man. I wish I could help you." John Brown heard
the call. He turned and looked at her. Tears were in
his eyes.

He rode to the scaffold in a furniture wagon. He sat
on his own coffin. Beside the driver was the undertaker.

**John Brown kissing a slave woman's child
as he leaves the jail for his execution.**

Soldiers on horseback rode ahead, behind, and beside the wagon.

On the half-mile ride Brown talked with Captain Avis. At one time he said, "I can endure almost anything but parting from friends; that is very hard."

He also said, "It has been a characteristic of mine, from infancy, not to suffer from physical fear. I have suffered a thousand times more from bashfulness than from fear."

At the scaffold he stepped down from the wagon, having to be helped because of his chains. A reporter later described the scene: "He cast his eyes over the beautiful landscape, and followed the windings of the Blue Ridge Mountains in the distance. He looked up earnestly at the sun, and sky, and all about, and then remarked, 'This is a beautiful country.'"

On the scaffold he looked about. He said, "I see no citizens here—where are they?"

John Brown rides on his coffin to the gallows.

"The citizens are not allowed to be present—none but the troops" was the reply.

"That ought not to be," he said. "Citizens should be allowed to be present as well as others."

An eyewitness wrote, "There is no faltering in his step, but firmly and erect he stands amid the almost breathless lines of soldiery that surround him."

And another said, "I know that everyone within view was greatly impressed with the dignity of his bearing. I have since heard Southerners say that his courageous fortitude filled them with amazement."

Finally, with the noose around his neck, with the white cap over his head, he was led to stand on the trapdoor.

"I am ready at any time," he said, "but do not keep me needlessly waiting."

For some reason, cruel as it may seem, the man was kept waiting for more than ten minutes while the soldiers were shifted backward and forward under shouted commands.

Finally the order was given. The rope was cut with a hatchet. The trap fell. After twenty minutes the body was examined by physicians. It was lifted from the scaffold and placed in the coffin. The guard closed in, the cavalry led the return march of the mournful procession, and the body was taken to Harpers Ferry where Mrs. Brown was waiting. It was put on a train for Baltimore, Philadelphia, New York City, and on up, being transferred from one train to another. Later it was transported by wagon, by boat, and again by wagon to its final resting place in the shadow of a great rock on the farm in North Elba, some three hundred miles north of New York City.

On the morning of Thursday, December 8, 1859, members of the family and friends, black and white, gathered in the farmhouse for the funeral service led by the Reverend Joshua Young of Burlington, Vermont. The eulogy was delivered by the eloquent Wendell Phillips, who had accompanied Mrs. Brown as she brought the body back. He spoke of "that marvelous old man" who had "loosened the roots of the slave system."

Four of her daughters were seated with Mrs. Brown—Anne, Sarah, Ellen, and Ruth with her husband, Henry Thompson. Her son Salmon was there with his wife. Other sons who had survived did not dare to be seen in North Elba. The widows of Watson and Oliver sat with the widow of William Thompson.

Friends had brought boughs of evergreen and golden shafts of grain to express their sympathy. Blacks were there to mourn for the white man who had accepted them as friends and recognized them as equals.

Under a gray, sunless sky the body was taken out to the massive granite stone about fifty yards from the house. As the coffin was lowered into the grave, Lyman Epps, an ex-slave, with his wife and children, sang one of John Brown's favorite hymns.

> Blow ye the trumpet, blow
> Sweet is Thy work, my God, my King.
> I'll praise my Maker with my breath.
> O, happy is the man who hears.
> Why should we start and fear to die
> With songs and honors sounding loud
> Ah, lovely appearance of death.

John Brown is executed in a stubble

field near Charlestown, Virginia.

19

The Legend of John Brown

The legend that was John Brown did not begin with his execution on December 2, 1859. For many years Brown had been expressing in words and in deeds the hopes of the whole abolition movement. Most people were not willing to take up arms and march into battle to end slavery, but when news of the raid spread across the land abolitionists showed their approval.

The attack at Harpers Ferry dramatized the antislavery cause. It was widely reported in the press. Editors sent their best reporters to Virginia to gather details of the story and to cover the trials at Charlestown. The very words of John Brown were printed. They were quoted over and over, in the South as well as in the North.

Reaction to the news varied widely.

In the North, where antislavery sentiment was strong, some endorsed Brown's use of force, but from the news accounts of that day it is clear that most people considered the action as ill conceived and useless. The loss

of life was abhorred. Many Northerners agreed with
Southerners that the raid was an act of treason.

The *New York Times* wrote:

> While our people do unquestionably respect the per-
> sonal qualities of sincerity, consciousness and courage
> which Brown has displayed, not one in a hundred of
> them has the slightest sympathy with his invasion or
> fails to brand it as a high crime against Virginia, the
> peace of the community and the dictates of conscience
> and common sense.

In the South the raid was taken as evidence that Northerners were ready to destroy slavery by any means available. It strengthened the arguments of those who said
that southern states would have to withdraw, or secede,
from the Union.

The *Register* of Raleigh, North Carolina, had this to
say:

> The outbreak at Harpers Ferry and the disclosures con-
> sequent thereon, the dangerous character of public sen-
> timent in the North as manifested by the tone of the
> press and pulpit, lead unerringly to the conclusion that
> the election of a Black Republican* to the Presidency
> is probable, and we must infer that it would be the
> signal for immediate secession of the South from the
> Union. To suppose that the states of the South would
> submit to see one of these aiders and abettors of trea-
> son, murder, and robbery placed at the head of govern-
> ment, to see him placed in the commander-in-chiefship
> of the army and navy, invested with the control of armor-

---

* A candidate who was opposed to slavery.

ies, with the national treasury within his grasp and all
the national property under the control of himself and
his partisans, is to suppose that the South has run mad-
der than Old Brown himself is alleged to be and to
suppose what will never occur. No! The South will
never submit.

James Buchanan, who was president of the United
States at that time, wrote later that

the raid of John Brown made a deeper impression on
the Southern mind against the Union than all former
events. Considered merely as the isolated act of a desperate fanatic, it would have had no lasting effect. It
was the enthusiastic and permanent approbation of the
object of his expedition by the Abolitionists of the
North which spread alarm and apprehension throughout the South.

News of the raid and the eyewitness accounts of the
trial climaxed in the execution of John Brown just forty-
seven days after Brown and his men took their first prisoners as they entered Harpers Ferry. On that day bells
tolled in mourning across the land. Memorial services
were held in cities from Boston, Massachusetts, to Lawrence, Kansas. Prayers were offered. Hymns were sung.
New poems were written. Men rededicated themselves
to the cause of liberty.

The solemn memorial service in Albany, New York,
was repeatedly interrupted by the booming of a hun-
dred-gun salute.

Perhaps it was in Ohio that the most widespread dem-
onstrations took place. Public offices, banks, and other
business houses were closed in Akron. In Cleveland a

banner stretched across Superior Street quoted, "I cannot better serve the cause I love than to die for it."

Frederick Douglass, who had tried to persuade Brown to give up the idea of the raid, was on the day of the execution aboard a steamer bound for the safety of England. He later said of Brown, "His zeal in the cause of my race was far greater than mine. I could live for the slave but he could die for him."

Ralph Waldo Emerson said through his tears that the execution "made the gallows glorious like the cross."

The eloquent Reverend Theodore Parker lay dying in Rome. He had used his powers to promote the abolition cause in general and to support John Brown as its principal activist. He wrote of Brown's death, "The road to heaven is as short from the gallows as from a throne."

William Lloyd Garrison was one with whom Brown had disagreed because Garrison believed in a nonviolent program to promote abolition. Yet Garrison had always believed in Brown's sincerity. At Tremont Temple in Boston on the day of Brown's execution, Garrison pointed out that although he had labored all his life for peace he was now prepared to say, "Success to every slave insurrection in the South and in every slave country."

With the execution the John Brown legend became more firmly established.

There were few, if any, in America who did not know about him. In the North even those who doubted his wisdom admired his courage, and in the South those who scorned him as a fanatic recognized his influence.

The United States Senate appointed a committee to

investigate the Harpers Ferry affair. The committee put out writs of summons and warrants for arrest. Brown's close associates, like Frederick Douglass, were afraid that they would be prosecuted.

Mary Ellen Pleasant had written letters to him after she went to Harpers Ferry from Chatham. She had tried to persuade him not to attack the government installations there. She never gave him the $30,000. At the time of the raid she was hiding in Missouri.

Franklin Sanborn took refuge in Canada. Later, when he returned to Boston he was arrested on a warrant issued by the Senate. He escaped only after a mob of angry citizens attacked the arresting officers.

George Stearns accepted the summons of the committee. Under questioning he affirmed his support and faith in Brown, saying, "I believe John Brown to be the representative man of this century as Washington was of the past."

The wealthy Gerrit Smith broke down completely. As he was being taken off to a mental hospital, he insisted that he was going to Virginia to stand with John Brown.

And in the South rumors of slave insurrections persisted. Before the executions Governor Wise had received many reports of plans to free Brown and his men. It is true that some such plans were made. It is also true that Brown himself refused to cooperate with the planners. In fact, he said that by dying he would be more valuable to the cause of freedom than he could possibly be by living any longer.

After the execution strangers from the North were suspect. Virginia banned mail delivery of the *New York Tribune,* saying it was an abolitionist sheet. Reportedly a minister in Texas who criticized slavery in one of his sermons was given sixty lashes, and in South Carolina a man was lynched as one of Brown's associates.

The John Brown legend began with the fighting in Kansas; it developed around the raid and the executions in Virginia. It came to full strength as the Union broke in civil war and men marched into battle singing

> John Brown's body lies a mouldering in the grave
> But his soul goes marching on.
>
> Glory, glory, hallelujah!

The John Brown Song

In the spring of 1861 a quartet of soldiers in the Boston Light Infantry sang the song. It was to the tune of an old camp meeting number, "Say, Brother, Will You Meet Us?"

The regiment learned it and later sang it as they marched past the place where Crispus Attucks fell in Boston Common. Others sang the song. Bands played the tune. Soldiers sang it in Cairo, Illinois, in the fall of 1861. The words, as set down by the Reverend William W. Patton, pastor of Chicago's First Congregational Church, were published in the *Chicago Tribune* on December 16, 1861. There are many different versions of this song.

Old John Brown's body lies moldering in the grave,
While weep the sons of bondage whom he ventured
all to save;
But tho he lost his life while struggling for the slave,
His soul is marching on.

Chorus:

Glory, glory, hallelujah!
Glory, glory, hallelujah!
Glory, glory, hallelujah!
His soul is marching on.

Other verses, published and unpublished, include:

He captured Harpers Ferry, with his nineteen men
so few,
And frightened "Old Virginny" till she trembled
through and through;
They hung him for a traitor, themselves a traitor
crew,
But his soul is marching on.

and

John Brown was John the Baptist of the Christ we
are to see,
Christ who of the bondmen shall the liberator be,
And soon throughout the Sunny South the slaves
shall all be free,
For his soul is marching on.

Books for Further Reading

Abels, Jules. *Man on Fire: John Brown and the Cause of Liberty.* New York: Macmillan, 1971.

Anderson, Osborn P. *A Voice From Harpers Ferry.* Originally printed for the author. Boston, 1861. Reprint. New York: Arno Press, 1972.

Barry, Joseph. *The Strange Story of Harpers Ferry.* Martinsburg, West Virginia: Thompson Brothers, 1903. Reprint. Shepherdstown, West Virginia: The Shepherdstown Press, 1958.

Boyer, Richard O. *The Legend of John Brown: A Biography and a History.* New York: Alfred A. Knopf, 1973.

Branch, William. *In Splendid Error, A Play in Three Acts.* In the collection *Black Theater.* New York: Dodd, Mead, 1971. First presented at Greenwich Mews Theater in New York, October 26, 1954.

Daingerfield, John E.P. "John Brown at Harpers Ferry." *Century Magazine,* vol. 16 (June 1885).

Douglass, Frederick. *The Life and Times of Frederick Douglass.* Boston: DeWolfe, Fiske and Co., 1892. Adapted by Barbara Ritchie reprint. New York: Thomas Y. Crowell, 1966.

DuBois, W. E. Burghardt. *John Brown.* Philadelphia: George W. Jacobs and Co., 1909. Rev. ed. New York: International Publishers, 1962.

Graham, Lorenz. *John Brown's Raid: A Picture History of the Attack on Harpers Ferry, Virginia.* New York: Scholastic Book Services, 1972.

Graham, Shirley. *There Was Once a Slave.* New York: Julian Messner, 1947.

Hinton, Richard Josiah. *John Brown and His Men.* New York: Funk and Wagnalls, 1894. Reprint. New York: Arno Press, 1968.

Holdredge, Helen. *Mammy Pleasant.* New York: G. P. Putnam's Sons, 1953.

Oates, Stephen B. *To Purge This Land With Blood: A Biography of John Brown.* New York: Harper & Row, 1970.

Quarles, Benjamin. *Black Abolitionists.* New York: Oxford University Press, 1969.

Redpath, James. *The Public Life of Captain John Brown.* Boston: Thayer and Eldridge, 1860. Reprint. Freeport, N.Y.: Books for Libraries, 1970.

Ruchames, Louis. *A John Brown Reader.* New York: Grosset & Dunlap, 1959.

Sanborn, Franklin Benjamin. *The Life and Letters of John Brown, Liberator of Kansas and Martyr of Virginia.* Boston: Roberts Brothers, 1885. Reprint. New York: Negro Universities Press, 1969.

Von Holst, Hermann. *John Brown.* Boston: Cupples & Hurd, 1888.

Index

Page numbers in *italics* refer to illustrations.

[174]